The New Traditional Egalitarian Passover Haggadah

By Leona S. Green

Norlee Publishing Ltd.
South Euclid, Ohio

Revised edition: Copyright © Leona S. Green, 2015
First edition: Copyright © Leona S. Green, 2002

All rights reserved. No part of this book may be reproduced or transmitted in any form or by any means, electronic or mechanical, including photocopying, recording, or by any information storage and retrieval system, without written consent of the author.

Library of Congress Catalog Card Number: 00-103863
ISBN 978-0-9700927-2-5

Distributed by:

Norlee Publishing, Ltd.
P. O. Box 21504
South Euclid, OH 44121-0504
Tel/Fax. 216-381-7242
Email: norleepub@gmail.com

Printed in the United States of America

Passover Haggadah Hebrew lettering typeface, Frank Ruhl

Page 111 constitutes an extension of this copyright page.

 # Acknowledgments

I would like to thank a few very special people for their support and help during the writing of The Traditional Egalitarian Passover Haggadah. First, I must thank my aunt and uncle, Esther and Marcus Susman, of blessed memory, who taught my family and me the importance of Passover and the Seders. They created a special attitude and loving environment that we strive to duplicate in our own home.

Next, I want to thank a few individuals who gave freely of their friendship and expertise when I needed them. Dr. Rita Margolies was God's answer to my prayer for a miracle. She formatted this text. Dr. Hanoch McCarty's sensitivity and humaneness first made me aware of the need for this Haggadah. E. Ramonia Longs has been my role model for integrity, honesty and wisdom. Judy and Marshall Rosenberg have been generous beyond measure in their unqualified support. Charlotte Z. Gould contributed some extraordinary art, as did the students from Agnon School in Beachwood, Ohio. Carolyn Javitch, Shalom Romm and Audrey Katzman helped me with some of the computer technicalities of an earlier version. My niece, Rosalyn Richman, proofread the Haggadah and offered many suggestions that helped refine the text. My sister, Selma Ryave, and her late husband, Sam, attended all our Seders and lent their loving support and presence to the emergence of this Haggadah. My cousins, Zipporah, Klara, Shalom, of blessed memory, Keren, Zeev and Zohar Romm were the catalysis for the abridged sections.

To Rabbi Isadore Pickholtz, of blessed memory, and Dr. David Salczer, I am indebted for their patience, guidance and technical advice; they were never too busy to listen and help.

Finally, it is with deep love that I thank my husband Norman, of blessed memory; my children: Lynn, Ronna, Marc, Yehudis, Rabbi Eli; and my grandchildren: Esther, Moshe, Eliezer, Devorah, Gavriel, Chaya, Mendel, Shlomo, Rivka, Dov Ber, Yetta, Remy, Michael; and great grandchildren. They were the motivational force and the inspiration behind the years I spent putting this Haggadah together. It is to them, my family, that I dedicate this Haggadah. It is for them, and for all Jewish families, that we tell and retell the story of the Exodus.

> "God, how much You have given me. How much that was beautiful and how much that was hard to bear. Yet whenever I showed myself ready to bear it, the hard was directly transformed into the beautiful."
> *An Interrupted Life: The Diaries of Etty Hillesum 1941-1943*

Preface

My purpose in writing **The New Traditional Egalitarian Passover Haggadah** was threefold. Primarily, I wanted to acknowledge the presence of our foremothers, as well as our forefathers, in the history of our people. I attempted to achieve this through the use of egalitarian (gender-inclusive) language and narration that includes the historic roles our foremothers played in the drama of the Exodus. In the case of language modification, for example, I substituted "ancestors" for "forefathers." Further, in Hebrew, He/Him are considered neuter gender when referring to God; in English, they are not. Therefore, in some instances, I substituted the neuter English pronoun "You" for "He/Him" when referring to the Eternal.

Secondly, I strived meticulously to adhere to the traditional text and format (except as mentioned above), using background information to clarify meaning. The format is enhanced with some inspirational contemporary passages that can be used and included at the discretion of the individual(s) conducting the Seder.

Finally, I included explicit directions for conducting the Seder, so that those who wish to conduct a more traditional Seder, but who do not have the background, can do so. The gray areas create an abridged version that contains the essential elements of a Haggadah but is short enough to engage and hold the interest of the children present.

This Haggadah is, by no means, the complete and ultimate source of information for conducting a Seder. If there is any question in your mind concerning any aspect of the Seder or Passover, please consult your Rabbi.

 # How to Use This Haggadah

In the Hebrew transliteration:
Consonants are read as they sound in English except:

(ח, כ, ך)   which are pronounced as the *ch* in **challah**.

(א, ע) the silent Hebrew letters are not represented.

The vowels are pronounced as follows:

a	as in	about
e	as in	end
i	as in	bin
o	as in	go
u	as in	lunar
ai	as in	aisle
ei	as in	vein

A dash between vowels indicates that they do not form a diphthong and are pronounced separately:

pa-am

An apostrophe indicates a break in the pronunciation (the end of a syllable):

v'tocho

Direct instructions for conducting specific parts of the Seder will appear in *italics* preceded by the word "***Directions***."

> **Paragraphs indented on the left and right** indicate **background information** that clarifies the meaning and understanding of a particular section of the text and can be included in the Seder at the discretion of the leader(s).

> **Boxed text** identifies an **inspirational passage**—a contemporary selection to enrich the Passover experience. It can be included in the Seder at the discretion of the leader(s).

Gray text identifies the **essential elements** of the Haggadah in **abridged form**—a Haggadah within a Haggadah.

v

Preparation

The family begins Seder preparations weeks in advance. In accordance with the command, "There shall be no leaven seen in your home" *(Ex. 13:7)*, the house is thoroughly cleaned in all areas that might contain *chametz* (leaven) and a separate area is designated for the storing of *chametz*. Dishes for Passover are readied and stoves, sinks, refrigerators and counters are cleaned.

> Somewhere in the midst of the 'drudgery,' I learn the lesson of Passover, not only in my gut, but also in my muscles and bones. The deeper lesson of Passover is about transformation. At Rosh Hashanah, I think about all the ways I didn't live up to my ideals in the year that has passed, and I realize that I must change. At Passover, I look at my house, transformed and gleaming, and know that I **can** change. I can help to transform the world, and however slowly, I can transform myself.
>
> *Judy Petsonk (Excerpted from "Seder holds lesson for all of us," Cleveland Plain Dealer, April 11, 1998)*

Below are some notes on "Preparation for Passover" from **The Haggadah of Passover** translated by Abraham Regelson and **CELEBRATION: Pesah** by Women's League for Conservative Judaism. Some other helpful references for Passover preparation are **The Passover Haggadah, MeAm Lo'ez** (Culi) translated by Rabbi Aryeh Kaplan and **How to Run a Traditional Jewish Household** by Blu Greenberg. <u>All other specific guidelines and details of the law and ritual concerning Passover preparation can be obtained through consultation with your Rabbi.</u>

The Great Sabbath

The Sabbath before Passover is known as the Great Sabbath (*Shabbat Ha-gadol*), particularly because the prophetic reading of that day is from *Malachi 3:23:* "Behold I will send you Elijah the prophet before the coming of the great and terrible day of the Eternal." Others believe that on the Saturday before the Exodus the Israelites prepared their lambs for slaughter and many miracles occurred for them then.

The Haggadah is read and reviewed on that Sabbath in preparation for the Seder. It is also customary on this *Shabbat Ha-gadol* for the rabbi to deliver a *d'rasha*, a lengthy discourse explaining the minutiae of the festival laws. Usually, this is delivered in the afternoon; hence, to many the Sabbath was called "great" because of the long duration of the discourse.

The Selling of Chametz   מְכִירַת חָמֵץ   M'chirat Chametz

We are forbidden to eat and/or derive any benefit from *chametz* during Passover. In order to comply with this regulation, it is the Jewish Law to give away or sell all our *chametz* before Passover to a competent Rabbi. The Rabbi, acting as an agent, draws up the proper legal documents to sell the *chametz* to a non-Jew for the duration of Passover. The sale must be completed before 10:00 A.M. of the day of the first Seder. If the first night of Passover begins on Saturday, then the selling of *chametz* must be completed on Friday. After Passover, the *chametz* reverts to its original owner.

Kashering Dishes

Utensils that have been used for *chametz* are put away and replaced by new ones, or by ones that are exclusively kept for Passover. Some pots, pans and dishes used during the year may be used on Passover only after undergoing a certain process called *Kashering*, i.e., "made fit for use on Passover."

a) <u>EARTHENWARE DISHES AND VESSELS</u> used throughout the year may not be used at all on Passover. However, fine translucent chinaware, which has not been used for more than a year, may be used if scoured and cleaned in hot water.
b) <u>UTENSILS USED ON THE FIRE</u>, such as spits and broilers, must be made red-hot before they can be used for Passover. All utensils to be *kashered* must be cleansed and not utilized for a minimum of 24 hours and then *kashered*.
c) <u>METAL POTS AND PANS</u> must be thoroughly scoured, completely immersed in boiling water, then filled with water that is allowed to boil over the rim.
d) <u>SILVERWARE</u> must be thoroughly scoured three times and then placed in boiling water.
e) <u>GLASSWARE</u> should be soaked in water for three days, changing the water daily. This glassware should be used only in an emergency.
f) <u>TABLES, CLOSETS AND COUNTERS</u>, if used with *chametz*, should be thoroughly cleaned and covered.
g) <u>OVENS AND RANGES</u> must be thoroughly scraped, cleansed and heated to a glow. Put self-cleaning ovens through the self-cleaning cycle.
h) <u>MICROWAVE OVENS</u> should be thoroughly cleaned. Then place a bowl of water inside and turn the oven on until the water boils and a thick steam fills the oven. A microwave oven that has a browning element or a convection oven selection is not recommended for use on Passover.
i) <u>DISHWASHERS</u> should not be used for a period of 24 hours. Then run a full cycle with detergent and an empty dishwasher.

j) <u>KITCHEN SINKS</u> should be thoroughly cleansed. Pour boiling water over a metal sink and place a new sink rack in a porcelain sink.
k) <u>REFRIGERATORS</u> should be thoroughly washed and emptied of all *chametz*.

The Fast of the Firstborn

The Fast of the Firstborn is a symbolic expression of Israel's gratitude to God for having spared the Jewish firstborn when the Egyptian firstborn were slain. On the day before Passover, all firstborn are to fast. As a substitution for this fast, they may participate in sacred study, in a *Siyum* or conclusion of a Talmudic tractate, held in the Synagogue on the morning before Passover. Thus the fast is made unnecessary while the purpose is enhanced. This illustrates again the high merit of study in Jewish life.

Food Guide for Passover

The distinction between leavened and unleavened applies only to bread or any other form of food prepared out of any of the following: <u>barley, wheat, rye, oats, and spelt</u>. **Bread or cake prepared from any of these is called unleavened bread (*Matzah*), if the dough is baked immediately after it has been prepared, no time being left for fermentation.** (It is only the fermentation of any of these kinds of grain that forms *chametz*). Fermentation of grapes or other fruit does not constitute *chametz*. It is, therefore, important to buy *Matzah* and *Matzah* products only from such people who are known and trusted to bake according to Law and under proper rabbinic supervision. The following are absolutely forbidden:

> Anything baked with yeast, soda (unless bottled under supervision), all cereals as well as foods prepared from wheat, barley, rye, oats, spelt and all liquids containing ingredients made from grain alcohol. In addition, *Ashkenazic* Jews (of European origin) do not eat rice, corn, millet, beans and peas.

The minutest amount of *chametz* found during Passover week, mixed with any other foods, renders all *chametz*. The rules of <u>Abstinence</u> and the care of the *Matzah* throughout all eight days of Passover must be strictly observed.

Some people abstain from eating *Matzah* for two weeks before Passover.

All articles made from flour, such as cakes and macaroons, need special supervision, as do canned goods, dried fruits, candies and flavored beverages. For a list of foods requiring no *kosher l'Pesach* label if purchased prior to Passover, and for foods requiring a *kosher l'Pesach* label before and during Passover, <u>check with a competent rabbinic authority when in doubt.</u>

Create Plague Bags

Prepare the "Plague" bags. Buy 10 small opaque reusable plastic bags. Number each bag from 1-10. Attach Velcro™ strips to the top of each bag for closure. Place the appropriate items in each bag.

Eruv Tavshilin עֵרוּב תַּבְשִׁילִין

Festival Cooking Exception for Sabbath

One is permitted to prepare food on a holiday only if it is to be used on that same day. An exception is made if the Sabbath occurs immediately after the holiday. Therefore, when the first Seder falls on a Wednesday or Thursday night, preparation for the Sabbath is symbolically begun the day of the festival before candlelighting. Some food (such as an egg, a piece of meat or fish) is cooked on that day and set aside with a piece of *matzah* to be eaten on the Sabbath. This act, along with the following blessings, permits the preparation of additional food for the Sabbath during the festival days.

Directions: Set aside a small quantity of food and recite:

Baruch Ata Adonai Eloheinu Melech Ha-olam asher kid'shanu b'mitz'votav v'tzivanu al mitz'vat eruv.

בָּרוּךְ אַתָּה יְיָ אֱלֹהֵינוּ מֶלֶךְ הָעוֹלָם, אֲשֶׁר קִדְּשָׁנוּ בְּמִצְוֹתָיו, וְצִוָּנוּ עַל מִצְוַת עֵרוּב.

Bahadein eruva y'hei sharei lana la-afu-yei u-l'va'shulei u-l'at'munei. U-l'ad'lukei sh'raga u-l'takana u-l'me'abad kol tzar'chana. Miyoma tava l'shabata lanu u-l'chal Yis'ra-el hadarim ba-ir hazot.

בַּהֲדֵין עֵרוּבָא יְהֵא שָׁרֵא לָנָא לַאֲפוּיֵי וּלְבַשּׁוּלֵי וּלְאַטְמוּנֵי וּלְאַדְלוּקֵי שְׁרָגָא וּלְתַקָּנָא וּלְמֶעְבַּד כָּל צָרְכָּנָא, מִיּוֹמָא טָבָא לְשַׁבַּתָּא לָנוּ וּלְכָל יִשְׂרָאֵל הַדָּרִים בָּעִיר הַזֹּאת.

Blessed are You, Eternal our God, Ruler of the universe, Who has made us holy through Your commandments, and instructed us concerning the *eruv*.

By means of this eruv (mixture), we are permitted to bake, cook, and warm food, light candles and do anything necessary on the festival in preparation for the Sabbath—we and all who live in this place.

B'dikat Chametz   בְּדִיקַת חָמֵץ   Search for Leaven

On the evening before the night of the first Seder (on Thursday night when the first day of Passover occurs on Sunday), the search for leaven, *b'dikat chametz*, begins. This custom symbolizes the final cleaning of all *chametz* from the house. Usually, ten well-wrapped pieces of bread are hidden in various rooms in the house before the search begins. The search is traditionally conducted with a candle (or other light source) and with a feather and wooden spoon to collect the *chametz*. The *chametz* is put in a paper bag and set aside to burn in the morning.

Directions: Before the search begins, recite the following:

Baruch Ata Adonai, Eloheinu Melech Ha-olam, asher kid'shanu b'mitzvotav v'tzivanu al bi-ur chametz.

בָּרוּךְ אַתָּה יְיָ אֱלֹהֵינוּ מֶלֶךְ הָעוֹלָם, אֲשֶׁר קִדְּשָׁנוּ בְּמִצְוֹתָיו, וְצִוָּנוּ עַל בִּעוּר חָמֵץ.

    Blessed are You, Eternal our God, Ruler of the universe, Who has made us holy through Your commandments and instructed us to remove all leaven.

Directions: Nullifying the leaven is called Bittul Chametz. After the search is completed and the leaven is put in a bag, recite the following:

Kol chami-ra vachami-a d'ika vir'shuti. D'la chamitei u-d'la vi-ar'tei. U-d'la y'da'na lei. Libateil v'lehevei hef'keir k'af'ra d'ar'a.

כָּל חֲמִירָא וַחֲמִיעָה דְאִכָּא בִרְשׁוּתִי, דְּלָא חֲמִתֵהּ וּדְלָא בְעַרְתֵּהּ. וּדְלָא יְדַעֲנָא לֵהּ, לִבָּטֵל וְלֶהֱוֵי הֶפְקֵר כְּעַפְרָא דְאַרְעָא.

    May all leaven in my possession that I have not seen or removed be regarded as non-existent and considered as mere dust of the earth.

Directions: The following morning, at about 9:00 A.M. (on Friday morning when the first day of Passover falls on Sunday), we add any remains from breakfast to the bag of chametz and burn it outside the home. The removal of leaven is called Bi-ur Chametz. This is the final act of removing chametz from the house. It is important to recite the final declaration in language that one understands.

Kol chami-ra vachami-a d'ika vir'shuti. Dachazi-teh u-d'la chaziteh. Dachamiteh u-dila chamiteh. D'vi-ar'teh u-d'la vi-ar'teh. Libatel v'lehevei hef'keir k'af'ra d'ar'a.

כָּל חֲמִירָא וַחֲמִיעָה דְאִכָּא בִרְשׁוּתִי, דַּחֲזִתֵהּ וּדְלָא חֲזִתֵהּ, דַּחֲמִתֵּהּ וּדְלָא חֲמִתֵהּ, דְּבִעַרְתֵּהּ וּדְלָא בְעַרְתֵּהּ, לִבָּטֵל וְלֶהֱוֵי הֶפְקֵר כְּעַפְרָא דְאַרְעָא.

    May all leaven in my possession, whether I have seen it or not, whether I have removed it or not, or whether I have burnt it or not, be regarded as non-existent and considered as mere dust of the earth.

The Leader(s)

THE SEDER is basically a shared experience, with each person an active participant. Nevertheless, it is a good idea for one or two people to assume responsibility for studying the Haggadah in advance and planning how it is to be used. The leader(s) is generally prepared to recite several basic portions, explain and coordinate the service while leaving some room for spontaneity.

The Seder Table

THE SEDER TABLE is attractively set. Spring flowers are appropriate, since Passover is also a Festival of Spring—*Chag Ha-Aviv*. The table is prepared for two consecutive parts: the first is the ritual of the Haggadah, while the second is the meal itself.

At the table, it is traditional for the leader(s) to have a Seder Plate (*k'arah shel Pesach*), a *Matzah* Cover with three compartments—each containing one *matzah*, a *Kiddish* cup, red wine, a bowl of salt water, a wine cup for Elijah and a water cup for Miriam. Identical Seder plates can be distributed around the table so participants may assist in dispersing the *Kar'pas, Charoset, Maror,* and *Chazeret*.

The meal is a learning and a religious experience, giving us the opportunity to serve God through blessings and prayers of thanks to the Provider of the food. However, the Seder table also represents a sacred altar in the Temple with the Passover offering lying upon it. "It binds the family and the community to each other, to their common past, and to their common future, as well as to their God." And the most important element of the meal is not the food, but the spiritual component that emerges from the *Div'rei Torah* (words of the Torah).[1]

SEDER by Craig Lynch
Heading East heading out — FREE
Creating the vision
On acts of inclusion
Making it so hard

I stood at the brink
Then paused to think
If I do take this trip
What's my role?
What's the script?

Thumbing wine-soaked pages
Scoping scenes of the ages
Seeking me in the crowd
Heads and spirits unbowed

Now the time is right
To put fear to flight
To take hold of wings
Soar above queens and kings

Then I'll know freedom's call
As it lifts one and all
Over time and space
Gives relief from the haste of a slave

Had'lakat Ner shel Yom Tov הַדְלָקַת נֵר שֶׁל יוֹם טוֹב

Blessing the Festival Candles

Directions: Before sunset and prior to sitting down for the Seder, the mother, daughters, and others who want to participate, light the candles and pray:

Our God and God of our ancestors, may these festival candles spread their light to every dark corner of the world. May the message of Passover fill our hearts and souls with a desire to bring freedom and peace to all people everywhere. Bless this holiday and inspire each of us with renewed determination to honor and bring goodness to ourselves, our family, our friends, our community and the world.

Directions: On the Sabbath add words in parentheses.

Baruch Ata Adonai, Eloheinu Melech Ha-olam, asher kid'shanu b'mitz'votav v'tzivanu l'had'lik ner shel (Shabbat v'shel) Yom Tov.

בָּרוּךְ אַתָּה יְיָ אֱלֹהֵינוּ מֶלֶךְ הָעוֹלָם, אֲשֶׁר קִדְּשָׁנוּ בְּמִצְוֹתָיו וְצִוָּנוּ לְהַדְלִיק נֵר שֶׁל (שַׁבָּת וְשֶׁל) יוֹם טוֹב.

Blessed are You, Eternal our God, Ruler of the universe, Who has made us holy with Your commandments and instructed us to kindle the (Sabbath and the) Festival lights.

Baruch Ata Adonai, Eloheinu Melech Ha-olam, she-he-cheyanu v'ki-y'manu v'hi-gi-anu laz'man hazeh.

בָּרוּךְ אַתָּה יְיָ אֱלֹהֵינוּ מֶלֶךְ הָעוֹלָם, שֶׁהֶחֱיָנוּ וְקִיְּמָנוּ וְהִגִּיעָנוּ לַזְּמַן הַזֶּה.

Blessed are You, Eternal our God, Ruler of the universe, Who has given us life, sustained us and helped us to reach this season.

Parental Blessings

(For sons:)

Y'sim'cha Elohim k'ef'rayim v'chim'nasheh.   יְשִׂמְךָ אֱלֹהִים כְּאֶפְרַיִם וְכִמְנַשֶּׁה.

    May God make you like Ephraim and Manasseh.

(For daughters:)

Y'simech Elohim k'Sara Riv'ka Rachel V'Le-ah.   יְשִׂמֵךְ אֱלֹהִים כְּשָׂרָה רִבְקָה רָחֵל וְלֵאָה.

    May God make you like Sarah, Rebecca, Rachel and Leah.

(A blessing said over all participants:)

Y'varech'cha Adonai v'yish'm'recha.
Ya-er Adonai panav elecha vi-chuneka.
Yisah Adonai panav elecha v'yasem l'cha shalom.

יְבָרֶכְךָ יְיָ וְיִשְׁמְרֶךָ. יָאֵר יְיָ פָּנָיו אֵלֶיךָ וִיחֻנֶּךָּ. יִשָּׂא יְיָ פָּנָיו אֵלֶיךָ, וְיָשֵׂם לְךָ שָׁלוֹם.

    May God bless you and keep you. May God smile upon you and be gracious to you. May God look upon you with favor and give you peace.

THE SEDER PLATE:
קְעָרָה שֶׁל פֶּסַח
K'arah Shel Pesach

Overlaying the Seder plate, the star and its points represent the following meaning according to Rabbi Isaac Luria, the Ari of Safed:

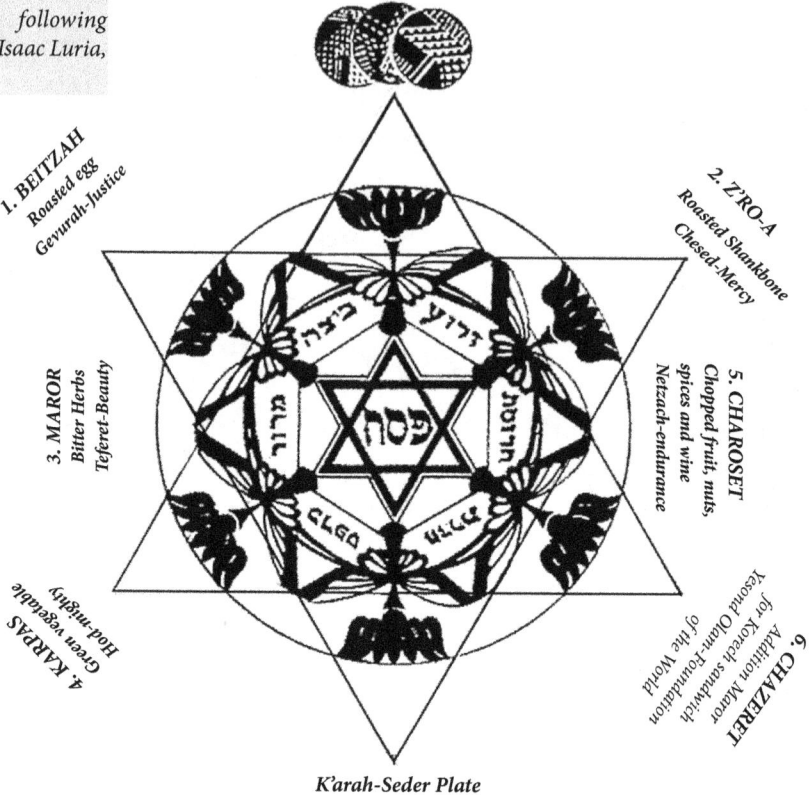

Three Matzot
Keter-Crown, Chochmah-Wisdom, Binah Intelligence

1. BEITZAH
Roasted egg
Gevurah-Justice

2. Z'RO-A
Roasted Shankbone
Chesed-Mercy

3. MAROR
Bitter Herbs
Teferet-Beauty

4. KARPAS
Green vegetable
Hod-majesty

5. CHAROSET
Chopped fruit, nuts, spices and wine
Netzach-endurance

6. CHAZERET
Addition Maror for Koreich sandwich
Yesod Olam-Foundation of the World

K'arah-Seder Plate
Mal'chut-Feminine Presence of God, Shechina

Directions: All sit down. This is a good opportunity for the leader to welcome everyone and explain how he/she will conduct the Seder and how guests may participate. At this point, the leader(s) may choose to explain and distribute the Maror, Kar'pas, Charoset, and Chazeret to each participant for later use.

1. Beitzah—The *Beitzah* is a baked or roasted egg symbolizing the festival offering, the *chagigah*, which was sacrificed in the days of the Temple. It symbolizes many things, among which may be grief for the destruction of the Temple, as well as the continuity of life and the very core of growth and renewal.

Directions: Some time prior to the Seder, place an unshelled hard-boiled egg over a lighted candle until a part is scorched.

2. Z'ro-a—The *Z'ro-a* means forearm. It symbolizes the Passover Lamb used as a ritual offering at the Temple and then eaten roasted at the Seder to commemorate the roasted Passover Lamb our people ate in Egypt the night they were freed. Some say it refers to God's forearm, which brought the Israelites from Egypt.

Directions: The Z'ro-a is a roasted shankbone, wing, or neck of a fowl with a little meat on it, burned or scorched.

3. Maror—The *Maror* refers to bitter herbs (either the core of romaine lettuce or the coarsely grated top part of the horseradish root). It is the symbol of the bitterness of slavery in ancient Egypt and in modern times. The *Maror* has a central position on the Seder Plate.

4. Kar'pas—The *Kar'pas* symbolizes springtime, the earth and the miracle of nature's renewal. Salt water symbolizes the salt water of the ocean and the bitter tears shed by the Israelite slaves in Egypt. Together they symbolize the world and the hope for its unity and harmony.

Directions: Kar'pas consists of parsley, lettuce, celery, potato, or any green herb. It will be dipped in salt water and eaten.

5. Charoset—The *Charoset* is a finely chopped mixture of fruit, nuts, spices and wine. It is intended to "soften" the bitterness of the *Maror* and serve as a reminder of the clay our ancestors used to make bricks to build for the pharaohs. A strip of cinnamon bark may be placed near the *Charoset*, further symbolizing the bricks without straw our ancestors were forced to make. The *Charoset* is neither raised nor lowered, and it is not explained in the Haggadah.

6. Chazeret—The *Chazeret* is additional *Maror* (grated horseradish) used for the *Korech* sandwich. The *Chazeret* symbolizes that the Israelites had become so degraded they had to beg in order to survive.[2] In remembrance of Hillel's opinion, we eat a *Matzah-Maror* sandwich after we have satisfied the command to eat the *Matzah* and *Maror* separately.

Matzah—When the Israelites hastily left Egypt, they had no time to bake ordinary bread with leaven (*chametz*). Therefore, as a remembrance, unleavened bread (*matzah*) is used on Passover. In addition to the two whole loaves traditionally used for the Sabbath and Festivals, on Passover we include a third *Matzah* for (what some say represents) the bread of poverty (*lechem oni*). The three *Matzot* also suggest the three traditional ranks in Jewry: Cohen, Levi and Israel. Some also set aside a fourth *matzah*, "The *Matzah* of Hope" (see page 21).

Why is there an orange on the Seder Plate? — It represents the evolving equality of women in Jewish Life as rabbis, teachers, students of Torah, and in all ways.

Directions: In front of the leader(s) and usually to the right of or below the Seder Plate, three Shmurah Matzot are placed in a special cover with three sections, or in a napkin folded over twice.

Shmurah Matzah — *Shmurah Matzah* is customarily used during the Seders. It is made from wheat flour and safeguarded against moisture from the time of harvest.

The Empty Chair — It is customary to leave an extra chair at the table symbolizing those of our people who live in lands where they cannot celebrate Passover as free Jews.

Reclining and Pillows — Some put a pillow on the left side of their chair for leaning. It is customary to recline during the Seder, since reclining was a sign of freedom in the ancient world. We recline to the left when we partake of the Four Cups, *Kar'pas*, *Korech*, and *Afikoman*. We do not recline for symbols of slavery, e.g., *Maror*, dipped in *Charoset*.

Kittel — In some households, the leader wears a white robe called a *kittel*. The white robe is a reminder of the garments worn on sacred occasions by the priests in the ancient Temple. White is also a symbol of joy, festivity and freedom.

Wine — *Kosher* for Passover wine is needed for the Four Cups. The wine cups should hold at least 3.38 fluid ounces.[3] If the Seder is on the Sabbath, the first cup should hold at least 4.42 fluid ounces.[4] It is best to use red wine as a reminder of the blood of the Jewish children killed by the Pharaoh. Since most of the wine must be drunk each time, children or people with health problems can drink *Kosher* for Passover grape juice.

The Four Cups of Wine — During the Seder we drink four cups of wine or grape juice. They remind us of four of God's promises for freedom from slavery and our gratitude for our redemption. And the four are:

- *Kadesh*— Prayer of Sanctification
- *Maggid*—Story of Exodus
- *Birkat HaMazon*—Blessing after Eating
- **End of Hallel**—Songs of Praise to God

The most widely accepted explanation of the Four Cups of wine at the Seder is related to four different Torah expressions that symbolize Israel's descent to Egypt and her ascent from bondage *(Ex. 6:6,7)*:

1. וְהוֹצֵאתִי V'ho-tze-ti, "**and I will take you out** from under the burdens of the Egyptians."

2. וְהִצַּלְתִּי V'hi-tzal'ti, "**and I will save you** from their bondage."

3. וְגָאַלְתִּי V'ga-al'ti, "**and I will rescue you** with an outstretched arm, and with mighty acts of judgment."

4. וְלָקַחְתִּי V'la-kach'ti, "**and I will take you** as My own people and you shall have Me as your God."

Debate over a possible fifth cup of wine will be discussed in the section on "The Cup of Elijah and The Cup of Miriam."

The Cup of Elijah and the Cup of Miriam—Two large fine cups are put in prominent places on the Seder table. They are not filled until the conclusion of the meal. Legend states that the Prophet Elijah visits each home during the Seder and drinks from his cup. "The Cup of Miriam" honors the Prophet Miriam and her importance in our story and history. (A more detailed explanation of "The Cup of Elijah and The Cup of Miriam" can be found on page 72.)

Music—Hebrew passages should be chanted whenever possible, since music is a significant part of the Seder.

The Haggadah—Haggadah means telling the story of the Exodus. It is related to the word, *V'higgad'ta (Ex. 13:8)* "and you shall tell your child" (the story of the Exodus). Our Sages said: "If three persons have eaten together and have not discussed Torah, it is as though they had eaten of the sacrifices to the dead. But if three persons have eaten together and have spoken words of Torah, it is as though they had eaten from God's own table." *(Pirkei Avot 3:4)* This is when the children learn that on our Passover journey/quest, we became a people of God whose primary purpose was/is to serve The Eternal.

Seder—This Hebrew word means the "order or progression of the service." The list consists of 14 different items, of which the meal is one. In many homes, the Order of the Service (*Kadesh Ur'chatz*) is chanted and serves as the introduction to the formal start of the Seder.

Simanei Haseder   סִימָנֵי הַסֵּדֶר   Order of the Service

Directions: Chant:
Kadesh, ur'chatz, kar'pas, yachatz, maggid, rach'tzah, motzi-matzah, maror, korech, shul'chan orech, tzafun, barech, hallel, nir'tzah.

Praise God for fruit of vine,
And you may drink one cup of wine.
In salt you dip some green.
Break the *matzah* in between.
Of three *matzot* on the tray,
Take one piece to hide away.
Read how God set Israel free,
Rescued us from slavery.

Matzah you bless and eat,
With bitter herbs, *charoset* sweet.
At last the meal takes place.
But before you say the grace,
Find the *Afikoman.*
Bring the supper to its end.
Then recite the psalms to praise,
Final thanks to God we raise.

Malcolm H. Stern

1. KADESH	קַדֵּשׁ	*Kiddush* (Sanctify God's Name).
2. UR'CHATZ	וּרְחַץ	Wash the hands.
3. KAR'PAS	כַּרְפַּס	Eat a green vegetable.
4. YACHATZ	יַחַץ	Break the middle *matzah*.
5. MAGGID	מַגִּיד	Tell the Passover story.
6. RACH'TZAH	רָחְצָה	Wash the hands.
7. MOTZI-MATZAH	מוֹצִיא מַצָּה	Eat the *matzah*.
8. MAROR	מָרוֹר	Eat the bitter herbs.
9. KORECH	כּוֹרֵךְ	Eat the *matzah* and *maror* together.
10. SHUL'CHAN ORECH	שֻׁלְחָן עוֹרֵךְ	The festival meal.
11. TZAFUN	צָפוּן	Eat the *Afikoman*.
12. BARECH	בָּרֵךְ	The blessing after the meal.
13. HALLEL	הַלֵּל	Recite the Psalms of Praise.
14. NIR'TZAH	נִרְצָה	Conclude the Seder.

Opening Prayer

The Passover celebration is at the very root of the Jewish soul. More than three thousand years ago, at this season, our people set out on a journey, which brought Israel forth from degradation to joy.

The Israelites were the first to rebel against slavery and to institute a profoundly religious holiday dedicated to freedom.[5] Passover teaches us that freedom must never be taken for granted. We must persistently struggle to preserve and advance the cause of freedom and human dignity for all people everywhere.

Passover comes to remind us that the family is the center of Jewish life. The Seder is celebrated not in a synagogue, but in the home. Every Jewish home becomes a sanctuary, every table an altar expressing gratitude to God Who freed us. And it is not a teacher who must impart our heritage to the child, but the parent who must answer the child's questions.

Passover teaches us that the Jewish home must extend hospitality to the lonely, the forsaken, the poor and the hungry—that before the family gathers around the table, the doors must be opened to the stranger.

Passover teaches us of the centrality of God in our history and in our lives.

The Haggadah says: "Whoever enlarges upon the story of the Exodus from Egypt, that person is praiseworthy." May each of us pour our own brand of wine into an ancient *Kiddush* cup that preserves and transmits our tradition to every generation.

IMMIGRANTS AND STRANGERS

Our world is changing at such a rapid pace that many of us feel like foreigners in our own land and in our own lives. And those of us who are parents wonder whether the values that we cherish will make foreigners of our children in turn.

What then can we teach our children that will remain a standard in this constantly changing world? The wisdom that is provided by our Jewish heritage offers three kinds of guidance to help our children. We can help them become positively identified as Jews. We can teach them the true nature of love and respect between husband and wife, parent and child. And lastly, we can imbue them with a consciousness and a willingness to sacrifice for the well being of others.

Through Judaism we can provide the answers and as parents we must provide the models from which our children shall learn.

Gary M. Klein (adapted)

1. Kadesh קָדֵשׁ   Sanctify the Name of God

Directions: It is symbolic of freedom and nobility to have someone fill your cup of wine at the Seder.

As with the Sabbath and all major holidays, we usher in Passover with the blessing over wine, a symbol of gladness and celebration. We sanctify the name of God and join with Jews everywhere to relive our ancient history of slavery, redemption and freedom. May we emerge from this experience with renewed determination to abolish inequality and injustice wherever it may exist. With the traditional words of the *Kiddush*, we praise Your Holy Name.

Directions: **On the Sabbath** *stand up, hold the cup of wine in your right hand, and add the following:*

Va-y'hi-erev va-y'hi voker, yom hashishi: Va-y'chulu hashamayim v'ha-aretz v'chol tz'va-am: Va-y'chal Elohim ba-yom hash'vi-i m'lach'to asher asah: va-yish'bot ba-yom hash'vi-i mikol m'lachto asher asah. Va-y'varech Elohim et yom hash'vi-i va-y'kadesh oto ki vo Shavat mikol m'lachto asher bara Elohim la-asot.

וַיְהִי עֶרֶב וַיְהִי בֹקֶר, יוֹם הַשִּׁשִּׁי:
וַיְכֻלּוּ הַשָּׁמַיִם וְהָאָרֶץ וְכָל צְבָאָם:
וַיְכַל אֱלֹהִים בַּיּוֹם הַשְּׁבִיעִי, מְלַאכְתּוֹ
אֲשֶׁר עָשָׂה, וַיִּשְׁבֹּת בַּיּוֹם הַשְּׁבִיעִי,
מִכָּל מְלַאכְתּוֹ אֲשֶׁר עָשָׂה. וַיְבָרֶךְ
אֱלֹהִים אֶת יוֹם הַשְּׁבִיעִי וַיְקַדֵּשׁ
אֹתוֹ, כִּי בוֹ שָׁבַת מִכָּל מְלַאכְתּוֹ,
אֲשֶׁר בָּרָא אֱלֹהִים לַעֲשׂוֹת.

There was evening and there was morning, the sixth day. Finished were the heaven and earth and all they contained. On the seventh day, God finished all the work that God had created, and rested. God blessed the seventh day and made it holy, for God then rested from all the work that God created.

Directions: **On week nights** *remain seated, hold the cup in your right hand, and* **begin here**. *Do* **not** *drink the wine yet.*

Baruch Ata Adonai, Eloheinu Melech Ha-olom, borei p'ri hagafen.

בָּרוּךְ אַתָּה יְיָ אֱלֹהֵינוּ מֶלֶךְ הָעוֹלָם,
בּוֹרֵא פְּרִי הַגָּפֶן.

Blessed are You, Eternal our God, Ruler of the universe, Who creates the fruit of the vine.

Directions: **On the Sabbath**, *add the words in parentheses.*

Baruch Ata Adonai, Eloheinu Melech Ha-olam, asher bachar banu mikol am, v'romimanu mikol lashon, v'kid'shanu b'mitz'votav. Vatiten lanu, Adonai Eloheinu, b'ahavah (Shabatot lim'nucha u-)mo-adim l'simcha, hagim uz'manim l'sason, et yom (haShabbat hazeh v'et yom) Chag Hamatzot hazeh. Z'man cherutenu (b'ahavah), mik'ra kodesh, zecher litzi-at Mitzra-yim. Ki vanu vachar'ta v'otanu kidash'ta mikol ha-amim, (v'Shabbat) u-mo-adei kod'shecha (b'ahavah uv'ratzon,) b'simcha uv'sason hin'chal'tanu. Baruch Ata Adonai, m'kadesh (haShabbat v')Yis'ra-el v'haz'manim.

בָּרוּךְ אַתָּה יְיָ אֱלֹהֵינוּ מֶלֶךְ הָעוֹלָם, אֲשֶׁר בָּחַר בָּנוּ מִכָּל עָם, וְרוֹמְמָנוּ מִכָּל לָשׁוֹן, וְקִדְּשָׁנוּ בְּמִצְוֹתָיו. וַתִּתֶּן לָנוּ יְיָ אֱלֹהֵינוּ בְּאַהֲבָה (שַׁבָּתוֹת לִמְנוּחָה וּ)מוֹעֲדִים לְשִׂמְחָה, חַגִּים וּזְמַנִּים לְשָׂשׂוֹן, אֶת יוֹם (הַשַּׁבָּת הַזֶּה וְאֶת יוֹם) חַג הַמַּצּוֹת הַזֶּה, זְמַן חֵרוּתֵנוּ, (בְּאַהֲבָה,) מִקְרָא קֹדֶשׁ, זֵכֶר לִיצִיאַת מִצְרָיִם. כִּי בָנוּ בָחַרְתָּ וְאוֹתָנוּ קִדַּשְׁתָּ מִכָּל הָעַמִּים, (וְשַׁבָּת) וּמוֹעֲדֵי קָדְשֶׁךָ (בְּאַהֲבָה וּבְרָצוֹן) בְּשִׂמְחָה וּבְשָׂשׂוֹן הִנְחַלְתָּנוּ. בָּרוּךְ אַתָּה יְיָ, מְקַדֵּשׁ (הַשַּׁבָּת וְ)יִשְׂרָאֵל וְהַזְּמַנִּים.

Blessed are You, Eternal our God, Ruler of the universe, Who chose us from among all peoples and exalted us among all nations, teaching us holiness through Your Commandments. With love You gave us, Eternal our God, (Sabbaths for rest,) festivals for gladness, holidays and seasons for rejoicing, among them (this Sabbath day and) this Feast of *Matzot*, the season of our freedom, a sacred gathering commemorating our Exodus from Egypt. For You have chosen us from among all peoples to make us holy. Blessed are You, Eternal, Who sanctifies (the Sabbath, and) Israel and the festive seasons.

Directions: **On Saturday night**, *continue with* **Havdalah**. **On other nights**, *continue with Shehecheyanu.*

Havdalah הַבְדָּלָה Separation

Directions: For Saturday night only. Lift hands to the light of the candles.

Baruch Ata Adonai, Eloheinu Melech Ha-olam, borei m'orei ha-esh.

בָּרוּךְ אַתָּה יְיָ אֱלֹהֵינוּ מֶלֶךְ הָעוֹלָם, בּוֹרֵא מְאוֹרֵי הָאֵשׁ.

Blessed are You, Eternal our God, Ruler of the universe, Who creates the light of fire.

Baruch Ata Adonai, Eloheinu Melech ha-olam, hamav'dil bein kodesh l'chol, bein or l'choshech, bein Yis'ra-el la-amim, bein yom hash'vi-i l'sheshet y'mei hama-aseh. Bein k'dushat Shabbat lik'dushat Yom Tov hiv'dalta, v'et yom hash'vi-i misheshet y'mei hama-aseh kidash'ta; hiv'dal'ta v'kidash'ta et am'cha Yis'ra-el bik'dushatecha. Baruch Ata Adonai, hamav'dil bein kodesh l'kodesh.

בָּרוּךְ אַתָּה יְיָ אֱלֹהֵינוּ מֶלֶךְ הָעוֹלָם, הַמַּבְדִּיל בֵּין קֹדֶשׁ לְחֹל, בֵּין אוֹר לְחֹשֶׁךְ, בֵּין יִשְׂרָאֵל לָעַמִּים, בֵּין יוֹם הַשְּׁבִיעִי לְשֵׁשֶׁת יְמֵי הַמַּעֲשֶׂה. בֵּין קְדֻשַּׁת שַׁבָּת לִקְדֻשַּׁת יוֹם טוֹב הִבְדַּלְתָּ. וְאֶת יוֹם הַשְּׁבִיעִי מִשֵּׁשֶׁת יְמֵי הַמַּעֲשֶׂה קִדַּשְׁתָּ. הִבְדַּלְתָּ וְקִדַּשְׁתָּ אֶת עַמְּךָ יִשְׂרָאֵל בִּקְדֻשָּׁתֶךָ. בָּרוּךְ אַתָּה יְיָ הַמַּבְדִּיל בֵּין קֹדֶשׁ לְקֹדֶשׁ.

Blessed are You, Eternal our God, Ruler of the universe, Who makes a distinction between the holy and the ordinary, between light and darkness, between the people Israel and other peoples, between the seventh day of rest and the six days of work. You distinguished between the holiness of the Sabbath and the holiness of the Festivals, and hallowed the Sabbath above the six days of work. You made Israel holy with Your own holiness. Blessed are You, God, Who distinguishes between the holiness of the Sabbath and the holiness of the Festivals.

Shehecheyanu   שֶׁהֶחֱיָנוּ   Who has sustained us

Directions: Recited both nights of Passover.

Baruch Ata Adonai, Eloheinu Melech Ha-olam, she-hecheyanu, v'ki-y'manu, v'higi-anu laz'man hazeh.

בָּרוּךְ אַתָּה יְיָ אֱלֹהֵינוּ מֶלֶךְ הָעוֹלָם, שֶׁהֶחֱיָנוּ וְקִיְּמָנוּ וְהִגִּיעָנוּ לַזְּמַן הַזֶּה.

Blessed are You, Eternal our God, Ruler of the universe, Who has given us life, sustained us, and enabled us to reach this season.

Directions: All drink the first cup of wine while reclining to the left. An explanation follows (page 23) for why we recline to the left.

2. Ur'chatz   וּרְחַץ   Wash the Hands (symbolic washing)

It is customary to wash the hands now without pronouncing the usual blessing, in preparation for eating the *Kar'pas* dipped in salt water. This is often done symbolically by the person(s) who conducts the Seder. In the days of the Holy Temple, the laws of ritual purity required washing the hands before eating any produce that had been exposed to certain liquids.

Directions: The leader(s) removes all rings, then takes a cup or pitcher of water and pours it over the right hand two or three times. Repeat the procedure on the left hand, and dry your hands

3. Kar'pas כַּרְפַּס   Eat a Green Vegetable

Ka'rpas symbolizes springtime and the miracle of nature's renewal. Yehudis Cohen wrote this poem while in Israel:

> The blue, blue sky was filled with
> billowy, pillowy, cottony clouds—and
> so too were filled the dreams of all
> who stood there.
>   And the green spring grass, dancing
> in the soft wind, called all to listen
> to the declaration of the passing of
> winter and to bring hope that new life
> would soon appear.

Directions: Distribute a green vegetable, dip in salt water and recite:

Baruch Ata Adonai, Eloheinu Melech Ha-olam, borei p'ri ha-adamah.

בָּרוּךְ אַתָּה יְיָ אֱלֹהֵינוּ מֶלֶךְ הָעוֹלָם, בּוֹרֵא פְּרִי הָאֲדָמָה.

> Blessed are You, Eternal our God, Ruler of the universe, Who creates the fruit of the earth.

Directions: Eat the Kar'pas.

4. Yachatz יַחַץ   Break the Middle Matzah

Directions: No word or blessing is spoken before Yachatz. It is a silent, reflective act. Break the middle of the three matzot into two pieces. The larger piece, known as the "Afikoman," is wrapped in a napkin and set aside. The smaller piece is replaced between the two whole matzot and used later for the Ha-Motzi. Customarily, the leader or children hide the Afikoman when the leader leaves the table to wash. Since the Afikoman must be eaten to conclude the meal, the Seder cannot continue until the Afikoman is "ransomed."

On the Sabbath, we use two loaves of bread as a reminder of the double portion of manna the Children of Israel gathered on the sixth day of each week, while traveling in the Wilderness.*(Ex. 16:22)* In honor of Passover, we add a third *matzah* to the Seder.

Matzah is a symbol of the poor fare (*lechem oni* — bread of affliction) we were given as slaves in Egypt. Even that simple fare is broken in half to stress the extreme poverty of our lives in bondage. Paradoxically, *matzah* is also the symbol of redemption. It is the food our ancestors ate while leaving Egypt in haste. It represents the faith of Israel in God as our Redeemer.[6]

5. Maggid מַגִּיד   Tell the Story of Israel's Redemption from Egypt

Directions: As a sign of hospitality, the door is opened to remind us that no Jew should be excluded when other Jews are celebrating within. Uncover the Matzot and raise the plate for all to see.

Ha lach'ma an'ya di a-chalu av'hatana b'ar'a d'Mitz'rayim. Kol dich'fin yeitei v'yechol, kol ditz'rich yeitei v'yif'sach. Hashata hacha, l'shana ha-ba-a b'ar'a d'Yis'ra-el. Hashata av'dei, l'shana ha-ba-a b'nei chorin.

הָא לַחְמָא עַנְיָא דִּי אֲכָלוּ אַבְהָתָנָא בְּאַרְעָא דְמִצְרָיִם. כָּל דִּכְפִין יֵיתֵי וְיֵכוֹל, כָּל דִּצְרִיךְ יֵיתֵי וְיִפְסַח. הָשַׁתָּא הָכָא, לְשָׁנָה הַבָּאָה בְּאַרְעָא דְיִשְׂרָאֵל. הָשַׁתָּא עַבְדֵי, לְשָׁנָה הַבָּאָה בְּנֵי חוֹרִין:

This *Matzah* symbolizes the bread of poverty our ancestors ate while they were slaves in the land of Egypt. Let all that are hungry come and eat with us! Let all that are in need of spiritual nourishment come and share this Passover celebration with us! Now we are here; next year may we observe Passover in the Land of Israel. This year we are still enslaved; next year may we be a truly free people.

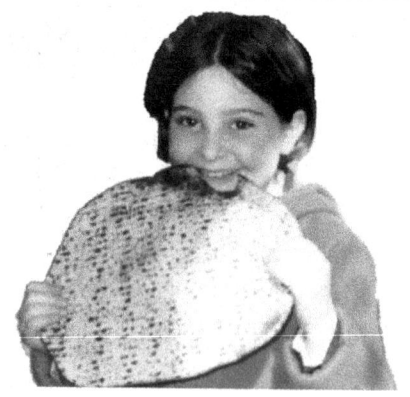

> We are commanded to renew our understanding of those days of long ago by imagining that we are the oppressed people who are not yet free. Let us here tonight dedicate ourselves to the struggle for freedom and resolve to strive untiringly until all share equally in the joys of Passover, poverty is no more, Israel is safe, and the chains that enslave all people are broken.
>
> We can be enslaved by our own emotions. When we permit harmful habits to tyrannize ourselves or others—we are slaves. When laziness, ignorance or fear blinds us to evil—we are slaves. When envy, bitterness and jealousy sour our joys and darken the brightness of our contentment—we are slaves to ourselves and shackled by the chains of our own making.
>
> We can be enslaved by materialism. When we choose to give up our Jewish way of life, to abandon our Torah, to neglect our sacred festivals, to ignore the rebuilding of our ancient homeland—we are slaves. These enslavements warp the spirit, blight the mind, and destroy the soul.
>
> Passover calls us to be free, free from the tyranny of our own selves, free from the enslavement of poverty and inequality, free from the corroding hate that eats away at the ties which unite all humanity. Next year may we be living in a new era of peace, love and reverence for all Jews and for all humanity.
>
> *Mordecai Kaplan, Eugene Kohn, and Ira Eisenstein (adapted)*

The Matzah of Hope

We set aside this fourth *Matzah* as a symbol of hope for the Jews of other lands who are not free to learn of their Jewish past or to pass it down to their children. It reminds us of their plight and unites us with them.

Directions: Close the door and cover the Matzot. Push away or remove the Seder tray to arouse the curiosity of the children and to encourage their questions and discussion. **Fill the wine cup for the second time.**

Ma Nish'tana מַה נִּשְׁתַּנָּה The Four Questions

The Four Questions touch upon the paradox of the Seder night, when the symbols of servitude and suffering intertwine with those of redemption. The *matzah* is slave bread but also a symbol of freedom. The bitter herbs are a symbol of servitude, but their use as an hors d'oeuvre dipped into another food is a sign of affluence. We eat *kar'pas* dipped in salt water to remind us of Jewish pain and tears, yet we recline as a sign of redemption.[7]

Directions: The youngest child or a guest asks the Four Questions now.

Ma nish'tana halaila hazeh mikol haleilot? (1) She-b'chol haleilot anu och'lin chametz u-matzah, halai'la hazeh kulo matzah? (2) She-b'chol haleilot anu och'lin sh'ar y'rakot, halai'la hazeh maror? (3) She-b'chol haleilot ein anu mat'bilin afilu pa-am echat, halai'la hazeh sh'tei f'amim? (4) She-b'chol haleilot anu och'lin bein yosh'vin u-vein m'subin, halaila hazeh kulanu m'subin?

מַה **נִּשְׁתַּנָּה** הַלַּיְלָה הַזֶּה מִכָּל הַלֵּילוֹת? [1] שֶׁבְּכָל הַלֵּילוֹת אָנוּ אוֹכְלִין חָמֵץ וּמַצָּה, הַלַּיְלָה הַזֶּה כֻּלּוֹ מַצָּה. [2] שֶׁבְּכָל הַלֵּילוֹת אָנוּ אוֹכְלִין שְׁאָר יְרָקוֹת הַלַּיְלָה הַזֶּה מָרוֹר. [3] שֶׁבְּכָל הַלֵּילוֹת אֵין אָנוּ מַטְבִּילִין אֲפִילוּ פַּעַם אֶחָת. הַלַּיְלָה הַזֶּה שְׁתֵּי פְעָמִים. [4] שֶׁבְּכָל הַלֵּילוֹת אָנוּ אוֹכְלִין בֵּין יוֹשְׁבִין וּבֵין מְסֻבִּין, הַלַּיְלָה הַזֶּה כֻּלָּנוּ מְסֻבִּין.

Why is this night different from all other nights? (1) On all other nights we may eat either leavened bread or *matzah*; why on this night only *matzah*? (2) On all other nights we eat other kinds of herbs; why on this night only bitter herbs? (3) On all other nights we do not dip the herbs even once; why on this night do we dip them twice: *kar'pas* in salt water and *maror* in *charoset*? (4) On all other nights we eat either sitting or reclining; why on this night do we all recline?

The Answers

Indeed, this night is very different from all other nights of the year. On this night we celebrate our ancestors' going forth in triumph from slavery into freedom.

Why do we eat only *matzah* tonight? Our ancestors fled Egypt in great haste taking unleavened bread dough with them. As they carried it, the hot sun beat down on the dough, baking it into flat bread, which they called *matzah*.

Why do we eat bitter herbs on Passover night? At the Seder, we eat bitter herbs to remind us of the bitterness our ancestors experienced when the Egyptian taskmasters oppressed them.

Why do we dip the herbs twice tonight? The vegetable reminds us of the green that comes to life again in the springtime, while the salt water reminds us of the tears shed by the oppressed Israelites. We dip the *maror*, or bitter herbs, in the sweet *charoset* as a sign that though our lives were made bitter with hard labor, with mortar and brick, we had the sweet promise of redemption that gave our ancestors strength.

Why do we recline at the table? In ancient times, slaves ate hurriedly, while standing or squatting on the ground, while the wealthy dined on couches. Since our people were freed on this night, we lean to the left when partaking of wine and symbolic food as a sign of our freedom.

We Jews are constantly reminded of our humble origins in order to understand that God works not only through nature but also through history. Our enslavement, the price of atonement our ancestors paid for the sin of selling Joseph, served to teach us the quality of kindness and mercy. Because of it, we were given the commandment concerning the freeing of slaves.[8]

When we chant the *Kiddush* on Sabbaths and Festivals, when we read the Ten Commandments, and especially when we say our daily prayers, we recall that God liberated our ancestors from slavery in Egypt. Reliving this experience helps us to appreciate freedom and strive to bring it to all people.

Directions: Now we return to the Haggadah text for the traditional answers to the Four Questions.

We were once the slaves of Pharaoh in Egypt, and our Eternal God brought us out from there with a strong hand and an outstretched arm. *(Deut. 6:21; 26:8)* If God had not brought our ancestors out of Egypt, then we, our children and our children's children might still be enslaved to Pharaoh in Egypt. Therefore, even if we were all wise, all full of understanding, and even if we were all sages and deeply learned in the Torah, it would still be our duty to tell and retell the story of the Exodus from Egypt. For the more we dwell on the story of the Exodus, the more praiseworthy are we and the deeper will be our understanding of freedom and our determination to win it for ourselves and for others.

עֲבָדִים הָיִינוּ לְפַרְעֹה בְּמִצְרָיִם, וַיּוֹצִיאֵנוּ יְיָ אֱלֹהֵינוּ מִשָּׁם בְּיָד חֲזָקָה וּבִזְרוֹעַ נְטוּיָה. וְאִלּוּ לֹא הוֹצִיא הַקָּדוֹשׁ בָּרוּךְ הוּא אֶת אֲבוֹתֵינוּ מִמִּצְרַיִם, הֲרֵי אָנוּ וּבָנֵינוּ וּבְנֵי בָנֵינוּ, מְשֻׁעְבָּדִים הָיִינוּ לְפַרְעֹה בְּמִצְרָיִם. וַאֲפִילוּ כֻּלָּנוּ חֲכָמִים, כֻּלָּנוּ נְבוֹנִים, כֻּלָּנוּ זְקֵנִים, כֻּלָּנוּ יוֹדְעִים אֶת הַתּוֹרָה, מִצְוָה עָלֵינוּ לְסַפֵּר בִּיצִיאַת מִצְרָיִם. וְכָל הַמַּרְבֶּה לְסַפֵּר בִּיצִיאַת מִצְרַיִם, הֲרֵי זֶה מְשֻׁבָּח:

Sing: **Avadim hayinu** hayinu, ata b'nei cho-rin, b'nei cho-rin, avadim hayinu, ata, ata, b'nei cho-rin avadim hayinu, ata, ata, b'nei cho-rin b'nei cho-rin.

The following passage, found only in the Haggadah, tells of a discussion held at a Seder by five outstanding Talmudic Sages in B'nei B'rak around 132 C.E. It is possible that they were planning the ill-fated Bar Kochba revolt against the Romans, who proclaimed the death penalty against those who studied the Torah. Rabbi Akiba, the greatest of the five scholars, and Rabbi Tarfon were martyred for the cause of freedom.

It is told that Rabbi Eli-ezer, Rabbi Yehoshu-a, Rabbi Elazar, son of Azaryah, Rabbi Akiba, and Rabbi Tarfon sat at the Seder table in the village of B'nei B'rak and, the whole night through, discussed the Exodus from Egypt until their students came in and said: "Rabbis! It is dawn and is now time to recite the morning Sh'ma."

Rabbi Elazar, son of Azaryah, who was only eighteen, said, "Though I am like a seventy-year-old man, yet I never understood why the story of the Exodus from Egypt should also be mentioned in the evening service, until Ben Zoma explained it by quoting the verse: 'That you may remember the day you went forth from Egypt all the days of your life.' *(Deut. 16:3)* 'The days of your life' would imply the daytime only. '**All** the days of your life,' includes the nights also." It is easy to remember our enslavement and redemption when all is well in our life. But we must also remember it all the days—even when our fortunes change, and the world becomes dark for us. The other Sages, however, explain it this way: "The days of your life refers to this world only. All the days of your life includes also the time of the Messiah."

מַעֲשֶׂה בְּרַבִּי אֱלִיעֶזֶר, וְרַבִּי יְהוֹשֻׁעַ, וְרַבִּי אֶלְעָזָר בֶּן עֲזַרְיָה, וְרַבִּי עֲקִיבָא, וְרַבִּי טַרְפוֹן, שֶׁהָיוּ מְסֻבִּין בִּבְנֵי בְרַק, וְהָיוּ מְסַפְּרִים בִּיצִיאַת מִצְרַיִם כָּל אוֹתוֹ הַלַּיְלָה. עַד שֶׁבָּאוּ תַלְמִידֵיהֶם וְאָמְרוּ לָהֶם: רַבּוֹתֵינוּ, הִגִּיעַ זְמַן קְרִיאַת שְׁמַע שֶׁל שַׁחֲרִית.

אָמַר רַבִּי אֶלְעָזָר בֶּן עֲזַרְיָה, הֲרֵי אֲנִי כְּבֶן שִׁבְעִים שָׁנָה, וְלֹא זָכִיתִי, שֶׁתֵּאָמֵר יְצִיאַת מִצְרַיִם בַּלֵּילוֹת, עַד שֶׁדְּרָשָׁהּ בֶּן זוֹמָא, שֶׁנֶּאֱמַר, לְמַעַן תִּזְכֹּר אֶת יוֹם צֵאתְךָ מֵאֶרֶץ מִצְרַיִם כֹּל יְמֵי חַיֶּיךָ. יְמֵי חַיֶּיךָ הַיָּמִים. כֹּל יְמֵי חַיֶּיךָ הַלֵּילוֹת. וַחֲכָמִים אוֹמְרִים: יְמֵי חַיֶּיךָ הָעוֹלָם הַזֶּה. כֹּל יְמֵי חַיֶּיךָ לְהָבִיא לִימוֹת הַמָּשִׁיחַ.

Ar'ba-ah Y'ladim אַרְבָּעָה יְלָדִים The Four Kinds of Children

Four times the Torah declares that parents should tell their children the story of Passover *(Ex. 12:26, 13:8, 13:14, and Deut. 6:20)*. But children are not all alike and each needs to be told the story of the Exodus in a different way. The Four Children symbolize traits that exist in each of us to varying degrees. As we read about each child, we can use this opportunity to examine these same positive and negative traits within ourselves.

Baruch Ha-makon Baruch Hu
Baruch Shenatan natan Torah
Shenatan Torah l'amo Yis-ra-el
Baruch Ha-makon Baruch Hu

בָּרוּךְ הַמָּקוֹם, בָּרוּךְ הוּא. בָּרוּךְ שֶׁנָּתַן
תּוֹרָה לְעַמּוֹ יִשְׂרָאֵל, בָּרוּךְ הוּא. כְּנֶגֶד
אַרְבָּעָה בָנִים דִּבְּרָה תוֹרָה: אֶחָד
חָכָם, וְאֶחָד רָשָׁע, וְאֶחָד תָּם, וְאֶחָד
שֶׁאֵינוֹ יוֹדֵעַ לִשְׁאוֹל.

Blessed is God Who gave us the Torah. The Torah speaks about four kinds of children. There is the one who is **wise**, one who is **rebellious**, one who is **simple**, and one who is **unable to ask**. Regardless of our wisdom, our age, or our knowledge, it is a religious obligation to tell the story of the Exodus from Egypt. Each child must hear the story—and deal with it on his/her own level of understanding.

Sing: The Ballad of the Four Children (Sung to Clementine melody)

Said the parents to their children, "At the Seder you will dine,
You will eat your fill of matzah, you will drink four cups of wine."
   Now these parents had two daughters and two sons, they numbered four
   One was wise and one rebellious, one was simple at his core.

And the fourth was sweet and winsome, she was young, and she was small
While her siblings asked the questions, she could scarcely speak at all.
   Said the wise child to her mother, "Would you please explain the laws
   And the customs of the Seder, will you please explain the cause."

And the mother proudly answered, "As our ancestors ate in speed,
Ate the paschal lamb 'ere midnight and from slavery were freed.
   "So we follow their example and 'ere midnight must complete
   All the Seder, and we should not, after twelve remain to eat."

Then did sneer the child rebellious, "What does all this mean to you?"
And the father's voice was anguished as his grief and anger grew.
   "If yourself you don't consider as a son of Israel,
   Then for you this has no meaning, you could be a slave as well."

Then the simple child said simply, "What is this?" and quietly
The good mother told her offspring, "We were freed from slavery."
   But the youngest child was silent, for she could not ask at all
   Her bright eyes were lit with wonder, as her father told her all.

Now dear children, heed the lesson, and remember ever more
What the parents told their children, told their children numbered four.

The Wise Child   חָכָם   Chacham

The **Wise Child** approaches life with a sincere desire to learn and to understand all, including the details. Teach this child that the taste of the *Afikoman (symbol of the Paschal lamb sacrifice)*, is the last food we put in our mouths all night. This reminds us that we become more spiritually connected to God whenever we perform *mitzvot* (good deeds) without regard for our own benefit. In this way, the pure spirit of the *mitzvah* is as undiluted[9] by our egos as is the *Afikoman* in our mouths. You shall explain that Judaism must be practiced as well as studied with humility.

The **Wise Child** asks, "What is the meaning of the symbols, rules and laws which our Eternal God has commanded you?" *(Deut. 6:20)* To this child you shall explain all the laws of Passover even to the last detail that nothing may be eaten and no entertainment shall take place after the *Afikoman*.

חָכָם מַה הוּא אוֹמֵר? מָה הָעֵדֹת וְהַחֻקִּים וְהַמִּשְׁפָּטִים אֲשֶׁר צִוָּה יְיָ אֱלֹהֵינוּ אֶתְכֶם? וְאַף אַתָּה אֱמָר לוֹ כְּהִלְכוֹת הַפֶּסַח: אֵין מַפְטִירִין אַחַר הַפֶּסַח אֲפִיקוֹמָן.

The Rebellious Child   רָשָׁע   Rasha

In the traditional explanation of the wicked, **rebellious child,** the child asks: "What does this service mean to you?" By using the expression "to you," it is evident the Passover Seder has little importance to this child, who finds the Seder upsetting and/or meaningless. The Haggadah tells us to use "tough love" with this child; "tough" because it is harsh on the child, "love" because it is applied out of concern for the child's welfare.[10]

But is this child, who has at least joined the family at their Seder, truly "wicked"? Although this scornful, despairing child turns away from God and Judaism, we must not turn away from him/her. We must confront this alienated child in a loving but direct manner, saying: "*Al tifrosh min ha-tzibur.* Do not separate yourself from the Jewish community." **Together** let us relearn and re-experience the joys and glory of our liberation from slavery.

The **Rebellious Child** asks, "What does this service mean to you?" *(Ex. 12:26)* To you, but not to me! And because this child excludes him/herself from the community, he/she denies God. To this child give a blunt answer and say, "It is because of what God did for **me** when I came out of Egypt." *(Ex. 13:8)* "For me, not for **you**, for had you been there in Egypt, you would not have been saved."

רָשָׁע מַה הוּא אוֹמֵר? מָה הָעֲבֹדָה הַזֹּאת לָכֶם? לָכֶם וְלֹא לוֹ, וּלְפִי שֶׁהוֹצִיא אֶת עַצְמוֹ מִן הַכְּלָל, כָּפַר בָּעִקָּר. וְאַף אַתָּה הַקְהֵה אֶת שִׁנָּיו, וֶאֱמֹר לוֹ: בַּעֲבוּר זֶה עָשָׂה יְיָ לִי בְּצֵאתִי מִמִּצְרָיִם. לִי וְלֹא לוֹ, אִלּוּ הָיָה שָׁם, לֹא הָיָה נִגְאָל.

The Simple Child   תָּם   Tam

In Hebrew, *tam* means "honesty and forthrightness." Rather than think of this child as uncomplicated, the tam can be thought of as religiously bewildered by the Passover ritual and, therefore, confused. If encouraged and given a satisfactory reason for a procedure, this child will do it.

The **simple child** asks: "What is this?" Tell this child, "With a mighty hand, God brought us out of Egypt, out of the house of bondage." *(Ex. 13:14)*

תָּם מַה הוּא אוֹמֵר? מַה זֹּאת? וְאָמַרְתָּ אֵלָיו: בְּחֹזֶק יָד הוֹצִיאָנוּ יְיָ מִמִּצְרַיִם מִבֵּית עֲבָדִים.

The Child Who Is Unable to Ask
וְשֶׁאֵינוֹ יוֹדֵעַ לִשְׁאוֹל
V'she-Eino Yode-a Lish'ol

The child who is unable to ask may be too young or, perhaps, lacking curiosity. Lovingly, we must attempt to encourage this child's curiosity and imagination, so that he/she will begin to ask.

As for the **one who is unable to ask**, open the discussion by explaining, as it is written: "You shall tell your child on that day, 'I do this because of what God did for me when I came out of Egypt.'" *(Ex. 13:8)*

וְשֶׁאֵינוֹ יוֹדֵעַ לִשְׁאוֹל, אַתְּ פְּתַח לוֹ. שֶׁנֶּאֱמַר: וְהִגַּדְתָּ לְבִנְךָ, בַּיּוֹם הַהוּא לֵאמֹר: בַּעֲבוּר זֶה עָשָׂה יְיָ לִי בְּצֵאתִי מִמִּצְרָיִם.

The Fifth Child

While the **Four Children** differ from one another in their reaction to the Seder, they have one thing in common: they are all present at the Seder. Even the alienated child is taking an active though rebellious interest in what is going on. We have hope that, some day, the alienated child might become a wise and conscientious Jew.

But in our time, there is another kind of Jewish child, a "**Fifth Child**," who is conspicuous by his/her absence from the Seder. This child has no interest whatsoever in our traditions and might not even be aware that tonight is the Seder. These children, through their own or parental decision, have chosen to assimilate into the environment by discarding the rich, beautiful heritage of their ancestors. They no longer belong to the **Four Children** of the Haggadah, even to the category of "simple" or "alienated."

Our ancestors in Egypt were a small minority who lived under the most difficult circumstances. Yet they preserved their identity with pride and dignity, clinging tenaciously to their own way of life, traditions and uniqueness. These acts of faith assured their continuing existence and eventually their deliverance from both physical and spiritual slavery.

May we all, each in our own way, show a **Fifth Child** the beauty, warmth, and uniqueness of Judaism and help him/her to become one of the **Four Children** once again.

Based on a 1957 letter of Rabbi Menachem Mendel Schneerson, Lubavitcher Rebbe of blessed memory

One might think you should begin to tell the Passover story on the first day of *Nisan* at the New Moon!*(Ex.13:8)* So the verse in the Torah adds, "on that day" the fifteenth day of *Nisan*—the day we actually left Egypt. Further, "on that day" could mean that we start the Seder in the daytime! Therefore, the Torah verse stresses, "Because of this, God did things for me when I left Egypt." *(Ex. 13:8)* That expression can only be used at night when the *Matzah* and *Maror* are placed before you and you can point to them.

יָכוֹל מֵרֹאשׁ חֹדֶשׁ, תַּלְמוּד לוֹמַר בַּיּוֹם הַהוּא. אִי בַּיּוֹם הַהוּא. יָכוֹל מִבְּעוֹד יוֹם, תַּלְמוּד לוֹמַר, בַּעֲבוּר זֶה. בַּעֲבוּר זֶה לֹא אָמַרְתִּי, אֶלָּא בְּשָׁעָה שֶׁיֵּשׁ מַצָּה וּמָרוֹר מֻנָּחִים לְפָנֶיךָ.

In the beginning, our ancestors were idol worshippers. But now God called us to serve the Almighty. As it is said: "And Joshua said to all the people: 'Thus said the Eternal, God of Israel: In olden times your ancestors lived beyond the Euphrates River; even Terach, the father of Abraham and Nachor, and they served other gods. Then I took your parents, Abraham and Sarah, from beyond the River and led them through the whole land of Canaan. I increased their family and gave them Isaac. To Isaac and Rebecca, I gave Jacob and Esau. To Esau, I gave Mount Se'ir as a possession; but Jacob and his children went down to Egypt.'" *(Josh. 24: 2-4)*

מִתְּחִלָּה עוֹבְדֵי עֲבוֹדָה זָרָה הָיוּ אֲבוֹתֵינוּ, וְעַכְשָׁו קֵרְבָנוּ הַמָּקוֹם לַעֲבוֹדָתוֹ. שֶׁנֶּאֱמַר: וַיֹּאמֶר יְהוֹשֻׁעַ אֶל כָּל הָעָם, כֹּה אָמַר יְיָ אֱלֹהֵי יִשְׂרָאֵל, בְּעֵבֶר הַנָּהָר יָשְׁבוּ אֲבוֹתֵיכֶם מֵעוֹלָם, תֶּרַח אֲבִי אַבְרָהָם וַאֲבִי נָחוֹר. וַיַּעַבְדוּ אֱלֹהִים אֲחֵרִים. וָאֶקַּח אֶת אֲבִיכֶם אֶת אַבְרָהָם מֵעֵבֶר הַנָּהָר, וָאוֹלֵךְ אוֹתוֹ בְּכָל אֶרֶץ כְּנָעַן. וָאַרְבֶּה אֶת זַרְעוֹ, וָאֶתֶּן לוֹ אֶת יִצְחָק. וָאֶתֵּן לְיִצְחָק אֶת יַעֲקֹב וְאֶת עֵשָׂו. וָאֶתֵּן לְעֵשָׂו אֶת הַר שֵׂעִיר, לָרֶשֶׁת אוֹתוֹ, וְיַעֲקֹב וּבָנָיו יָרְדוּ מִצְרָיִם.

Joseph, who was already in Egypt, emerged as prime minister to Pharaoh, King of Egypt. When a famine broke out in Canaan, Joseph asked his father and all his family to join him there. It was a good time for the Hebrews and they increased in number.

We now begin the core of the Haggadah. The Talmud states: "Begin with the degradation of our people and end with their glory." *(Peshahim 116a)* "Their glory" refers to the spiritual freedom our ancestors achieved when they received the Torah.

Blessed is God Who keeps promises to Israel! Blessed is God! For the Holy One, Who is blessed, planned the end of our bondage to fulfill the solemn covenant pledged to Abraham at the Covenant of the Pieces: "And God said to Abram,* 'Know for certain that your descendants shall be strangers in a land that is not theirs, where they shall be enslaved and oppressed four hundred years. But I will also judge the nation that held them in slavery; and in the end they shall go free with great wealth.'" *(Gen. 15: 13,14)*

בָּרוּךְ שׁוֹמֵר הַבְטָחָתוֹ לְיִשְׂרָאֵל, בָּרוּךְ הוּא. שֶׁהַקָּדוֹשׁ בָּרוּךְ הוּא חִשַּׁב אֶת הַקֵּץ, לַעֲשׂוֹת כְּמָה שֶׁאָמַר לְאַבְרָהָם אָבִינוּ בִּבְרִית בֵּין הַבְּתָרִים, שֶׁנֶּאֱמַר: וַיֹּאמֶר לְאַבְרָם יָדֹעַ תֵּדַע כִּי גֵר יִהְיֶה זַרְעֲךָ בְּאֶרֶץ לֹא לָהֶם, וַעֲבָדוּם וְעִנּוּ אֹתָם, אַרְבַּע מֵאוֹת שָׁנָה. וְגַם אֶת הַגּוֹי אֲשֶׁר יַעֲבֹדוּ דָּן אָנֹכִי, וְאַחֲרֵי כֵן יֵצְאוּ בִּרְכֻשׁ גָּדוֹל.

---

* After God promised Abram and Sarai to make them the parents of a multitude of great nations, God changed their names to Abraham and Sarah. *(Gen. 17.5, 15)*

Directions: Cover the Matzot to follow the rule that wine never takes precedence over bread (which represents God's miraculous gift of manna), and then raise the cup of wine in recognition of the eternal significance of the following paragraph:

V'hi she-am-dah, v'hi she-am-dah,
la-a-vo-tei-nu v'la-nu (repeat)
She-lo e-chad bil'vad
A-mad a-lei-nu l'cha-lo-tei-nu
   (repeat 2 lines above)
E-lah she-b'chol dor va-dor
Om-dim a-lei-nu l-cha-lo-tei-nu
   (repeat 2 lines above)
V'ha-ka-dosh ba-ruch hu
Ma-tzi-lei-nu mi-ya-dam.
   (repeat 2 lines above).

וְהִיא שֶׁעָמְדָה לַאֲבוֹתֵינוּ וְלָנוּ. שֶׁלֹא אֶחָד בִּלְבָד, עָמַד עָלֵינוּ לְכַלוֹתֵנוּ. אֶלָּא שֶׁבְּכָל דוֹר וָדוֹר עוֹמְדִים עָלֵינוּ לְכַלוֹתֵנוּ, וְהַקָדוֹשׁ בָּרוּךְ הוּא מַצִילֵנוּ מִיָדָם:

And that promise has been a source of strength to our ancestors and to us. For not only one enemy has risen up to destroy us; but in every generation, evil-doers rise up against us seeking to destroy us; but the Holy One, Who is blessed, rescues us from their hands.

Directions: Set the cup of wine down and uncover the Matzot.

This story reminds us that the "Labans" of this world are as great a threat to the survival of the Jewish people as the "Pharaohs." Pharaoh openly sought to oppress the Israelites who recognized his evil ways and feared him. But Laban outwardly appeared to be Jacob's friend, while inwardly he plotted to take Jacob's property, children, and life. While Pharaoh ordered the destruction of all male babies, Laban plotted to destroy everyone through assimilation. The Pharaohs of the world seek to annihilate us physically, while the Labans want our souls.

Go and learn what Laban the Aramean (Syrian) planned to do to our ancestors Jacob, Rachel and Leah. While Pharaoh decreed only that newborn males be put to death, Laban tried to exterminate everyone. As it is written: "An Aramean sought to destroy my father..." *(Deut. 26:5)*

צֵא וּלְמַד, מַה בִּקֵּשׁ לָבָן הָאֲרַמִּי לַעֲשׂוֹת לְיַעֲקֹב אָבִינוּ. שֶׁפַּרְעֹה לֹא גָזַר אֶלָּא עַל הַזְּכָרִים, וְלָבָן בִּקֵּשׁ לַעֲקוֹר אֶת הַכֹּל, שֶׁנֶּאֱמַר: אֲרַמִּי אֹבֵד אָבִי ...

Our story begins with degradation;
  Our telling ends with glory.

מַתְחִיל [לְהַגִּיד] בִּגְנוּת;
וּמְסַיֵּם [לְסַפֵּר] בְּשֶׁבַח.

An Aramean sought to destroy my family.
So they went down to Egypt, and lived there as strangers, few in number.

אֲרַמִּי אֹבֵד אָבִי, וַיֵּרֶד מִצְרַיְמָה,
וַיָּגָר שָׁם בִּמְתֵי מְעָט.

There they became a nation, great mighty, and numerous. *(Deut. 26:5)*

וַיְהִי שָׁם לְגוֹי גָּדוֹל, עָצוּם וָרָב.

But the Egyptians were cruel to us.
They made us suffer.

וַיָּרֵעוּ אֹתָנוּ הַמִּצְרִים. וַיְעַנּוּנוּ.

They imposed hard labor upon us. *(Deut. 26:6)*

וַיִּתְּנוּ עָלֵינוּ עֲבֹדָה קָשָׁה.

Then we cried out to the Eternal, the God of our ancestors.

וַנִּצְעַק אֶל יְיָ אֱלֹהֵי אֲבֹתֵינוּ.

And the Eternal heard our cry, saw our suffering, our woe, our oppression. *(Deut. 26:7)*

וַיִּשְׁמַע יְיָ אֶת קֹלֵנוּ, וַיַּרְא אֶת עָנְיֵנוּ, וְאֶת עֲמָלֵנוּ, וְאֶת לַחֲצֵנוּ.

Then God brought us out of Egypt
  with a mighty hand,
  with an outstretched arm,
  with awesome power,
  with signs and wonders. *(Deut. 26:8)*

וַיּוֹצִאֵנוּ יְיָ מִמִּצְרַיִם
בְּיָד חֲזָקָה,
וּבִזְרֹעַ נְטוּיָה,
וּבְמֹרָא גָּדוֹל
וּבְאֹתוֹת וּבְמוֹפְתִים.

The Exodus in Detail

The following ancient *Midrashic* interpretation of the four Torah verses above is found only in the Haggadah. In this section, background information may occur in parentheses as well as in indented paragraphs.

אֲרַמִּי אֹבֵד אָבִי
"An Aramean sought to destroy my family."

An Aramean tried to destroy my father, who went down to Egypt with a small family and lived there, becoming a nation—great, mighty, and numerous.

אֲרַמִּי אֹבֵד אָבִי, וַיֵּרֶד מִצְרַיְמָה, וַיָּגָר שָׁם בִּמְתֵי מְעָט, וַיְהִי שָׁם לְגוֹי גָּדוֹל, עָצוּם וָרָב.

> Jacob and his family fled from Laban, the false friend, who wanted to wean Jacob from the faith of his ancestors.

וַיֵּרֶד מִצְרַיְמָה
"So they went down to Egypt."

They were compelled to do so by Divine command.

וַיֵּרֶד מִצְרַיְמָה, אָנוּס עַל פִּי הַדִּבּוּר.

> The descent from Canaan to Egypt was also a spiritual descent, for our ancestors became important in the economy of Egypt and believed they had enough power and influence to be forever secure.[11] This is a recurring theme in our history.

וַיָּגָר שָׁם.
"They lived there as strangers."

This means that Jacob's family did not intend to settle there, but only to stay a short time. As it is written: "They said to Pharaoh, 'We have come to live in your land a while, for there is nothing even for our sheep to eat, since the famine is so great in the land of Canaan. And now, please let us, your servants, live in the land of Goshen.'" *(Gen. 47:4)*

וַיָּגָר שָׁם: מְלַמֵּד שֶׁלֹּא יָרַד יַעֲקֹב אָבִינוּ לְהִשְׁתַּקֵּעַ בְּמִצְרַיִם, אֶלָּא לָגוּר שָׁם. שֶׁנֶּאֱמַר, וַיֹּאמְרוּ אֶל פַּרְעֹה, לָגוּר בָּאָרֶץ בָּאנוּ, כִּי אֵין מִרְעֶה לַצֹּאן אֲשֶׁר לַעֲבָדֶיךָ, כִּי כָבֵד הָרָעָב בְּאֶרֶץ כְּנָעַן. וְעַתָּה, יֵשְׁבוּ נָא עֲבָדֶיךָ בְּאֶרֶץ גֹּשֶׁן.

> Though the Israelites planned to stay in Egypt only until the famine passed, God told Jacob that he must remain in Egypt because of their solemn covenant. "Know for sure your descendants will be strangers in a foreign land; they will be slaves there and treated harshly for four hundred years." *(Gen. 15:13)* The four hundred-year period should have begun from the time Jacob and his family migrated to Egypt. But God had mercy and began counting from the time that Isaac was born. The Israelites were, therefore, in Egypt for no more than 210 years.[12]

בִּמְתֵי מְעָט
"Few in number."

בִּמְתֵי מְעָט. כְּמָה שֶׁנֶּאֱמַר בְּשִׁבְעִים נֶפֶשׁ, יָרְדוּ אֲבֹתֶיךָ מִצְרָיְמָה, וְעַתָּה שָׂמְךָ יְיָ אֱלֹהֶיךָ כְּכוֹכְבֵי הַשָּׁמַיִם לָרֹב.

As Moses said to the children of Israel, "Your ancestors went down to Egypt with only seventy persons, but now, the Eternal, your God, has made you as numerous as the stars in the heaven." *(Deut. 10:22)*

וַיְהִי שָׁם לְגוֹי
"There they became a nation."

וַיְהִי שָׁם לְגוֹי: מְלַמֵּד שֶׁהָיוּ יִשְׂרָאֵל מְצֻיָּנִים שָׁם.

In Egypt, the Israelites were a nation who kept their own language and customs.

גָּדוֹל עָצוּם
"Great, mighty"

גָּדוֹל עָצוּם: כְּמָה שֶׁנֶּאֱמַר, וּבְנֵי יִשְׂרָאֵל פָּרוּ וַיִּשְׁרְצוּ, וַיִּרְבּוּ וַיַּעַצְמוּ, בִּמְאֹד מְאֹד, וַתִּמָּלֵא הָאָרֶץ אֹתָם.

As it is said: "And the children of Israel were fertile, prolific and multiplied, and they became great and mighty; the land was filled with them." *(Ex. 1:7)*

וָרָב
"And numerous."

וָרָב: כְּמָה שֶׁנֶּאֱמַר, רְבָבָה כְּצֶמַח הַשָּׂדֶה נְתַתִּיךְ, וַתִּרְבִּי, וַתִּגְדְּלִי, וַתָּבֹאִי בַּעֲדִי עֲדָיִים: שָׁדַיִם נָכֹנוּ, וּשְׂעָרֵךְ צִמֵּחַ, וְאַתְּ עֵרֹם וְעֶרְיָה.

As it is written: "I have caused you to thrive like the plant of the field. You grew tall, matured and reached beauty of figure. You were fully grown, yet remained naked and bare." *(Ezekiel 16:7)*

The Israelites had preserved their identity and grown in physical stature, but they were still spiritually immature, for they had not yet kept the commandments nor done good deeds.

וַיָּרֵעוּ אֹתָנוּ הַמִּצְרִים
"But the Egyptians were cruel to us."

As it is written: "Now a new king arose over Egypt who knew nothing of Joseph. He said to his subjects, 'Look how numerous and powerful the Israelite people are growing. Come let us deal shrewdly with them to stop their increase; otherwise, in time of war they may join our enemies, fight against us and drive us from the land.'" *(Ex. 1:8-10)*

וַיָּרֵעוּ אֹתָנוּ הַמִּצְרִים וַיְעַנּוּנוּ, וַיִּתְּנוּ עָלֵינוּ עֲבֹדָה קָשָׁה: וַיָּרֵעוּ אֹתָנוּ הַמִּצְרִים, כְּמָה שֶׁנֶּאֱמַר: הָבָה נִתְחַכְּמָה לוֹ, פֶּן יִרְבֶּה, וְהָיָה כִּי תִקְרֶאנָה מִלְחָמָה, וְנוֹסַף גַּם הוּא עַל שֹׂנְאֵינוּ, וְנִלְחַם בָּנוּ וְעָלָה מִן הָאָרֶץ.

A new ruler came into power, who chose to ignore the contributions Joseph and the Israelites made to Egyptian society. He was afraid the large number of Hebrews would turn against him. He shrewdly began to poison the minds of his own people against the Jews, who had become comfortable and secure in Egypt. Like so many other anti-Semitic tyrants throughout history, the Pharaoh accused the Jews of disloyalty and treachery.[13] He made slaves of the Hebrews, who were forced to work day and night to make bricks and build cities.

וַיְעַנּוּנוּ
"They made us suffer."

The Pharaoh put taskmasters over the Israelites and oppressed them with hard labor; thus they built supply cities for Pharaoh such as Pithom and Raamses. *(Ex. 1:11)*

וַיְעַנּוּנוּ: כְּמָה שֶׁנֶּאֱמַר, וַיָּשִׂימוּ עָלָיו שָׂרֵי מִסִּים, לְמַעַן עַנֹּתוֹ בְּסִבְלֹתָם, וַיִּבֶן עָרֵי מִסְכְּנוֹת לְפַרְעֹה, אֶת פִּתֹם וְאֶת רַעַמְסֵס.

The Egyptians lured us into slavery by trickery. Building the supply cities was presented as a high patriotic duty. All the Egyptians "volunteered," and on the first day, Pharaoh, himself, participated in the work. Seeing this, all the Israelites also signed up for conscription into the work force.[14]

On this first day, they all worked with great enthusiasm. Each one tried to make more bricks than the next to prove his patriotism. Meanwhile, Pharaoh's agents kept a careful tally of how many bricks each person was making. This became one's quota.[15]

It created endless work whose purpose was to degrade the Hebrews and break their spirit, not unlike what took place in Nazi Germany.

וַיִּתְּנוּ עָלֵינוּ עֲבֹדָה קָשָׁה.
"They imposed hard labor upon us." *(Deut. 26:7)*

As it is written, "The Egyptians made their lives bitter with hard labor with mortar and brick, and through all manner of labor in the field." *(Ex. 1:14)*

וַיִּתְּנוּ עָלֵינוּ עֲבֹדָה קָשָׁה: כְּמָה שֶׁנֶּאֱמַר, וַיַּעֲבִדוּ מִצְרַיִם אֶת בְּנֵי יִשְׂרָאֵל בְּפָרֶךְ.

Sing: "I've been workin' on these buildings," sung to the melody of "I've been workin' on the railroad."

I've been workin' on these buildings,
Pharaoh doesn't pay.
Workin' workin' on these buildings,
Oh it steals our pride away.
Can't you hear the Pharaoh calling,
"Rise up so early in the morn."
Can't you hear the Pharaoh calling,
"Slaves, Hebrews were born."

וַנִּצְעַק אֶל יְיָ אֱלֹהֵי אֲבֹתֵינוּ
"Then we cried out to the Eternal, the God of our ancestors."

As it is written, "During that long period, the king of Egypt died. The Children of Israel groaned under their bondage, and cried out; and their cry for help rose up to God from out of their bondage." *(Ex. 2:23)*

וַנִּצְעַק אֶל יְיָ אֱלֹהֵי אֲבֹתֵינוּ: כְּמָה שֶׁנֶּאֱמַר, וַיְהִי בַיָּמִים הָרַבִּים הָהֵם, וַיָּמָת מֶלֶךְ מִצְרַיִם, וַיֵּאָנְחוּ בְנֵי יִשְׂרָאֵל מִן הָעֲבֹדָה וַיִּזְעָקוּ. וַתַּעַל שַׁוְעָתָם אֶל הָאֱלֹהִים מִן הָעֲבֹדָה.

וַיִּשְׁמַע יְיָ אֶת קֹלֵנוּ
"And the Eternal heard our cry."

As it is written, "God heard their voices, and God remembered the covenant made with Abraham and Sarah, with Isaac and Rebecca and with Jacob, Rachel and Leah." *(Ex. 2:24)*

וַיִּשְׁמַע יְיָ אֶת קֹלֵנוּ: כְּמָה שֶׁנֶּאֱמַר: וַיִּשְׁמַע אֱלֹהִים אֶת נַאֲקָתָם, וַיִּזְכֹּר אֱלֹהִים אֶת בְּרִיתוֹ, אֶת אַבְרָהָם, וְשָׂרָה, אֶת יִצְחָק וְרִבְקָה, וְאֶת יַעֲקֹב רָחֵל וְלֵאָה.

וַיַּרְא אֶת עָנְיֵנוּ
"Saw our suffering."

This refers to the enforced separation of husbands and wives. As it is written, "And God saw the children of Israel and knew ... *(Ex. 2:25)*

וַיַּרְא אֶת עָנְיֵנוּ: זוֹ פְּרִישׁוּת דֶּרֶךְ אֶרֶץ. כְּמָה שֶׁנֶּאֱמַר, וַיַּרְא אֱלֹהִים אֶת בְּנֵי יִשְׂרָאֵל, וַיֵּדַע אֱלֹהִים.

The Egyptians decreed that the men should sleep in the fields and the women in the cities. But the women of Israel were a source of strength to their husbands, bringing them food and comforting them by saying, "We shall not be enslaved forever; the Holy One will free us." And though husbands and wives were kept separate, God made the Israelites increase "as if by a miracle."

"וְאֶת עֲמָלֵנוּ"
"Our woe (burden),"

As it is written, "Every boy that is born must be thrown into the river, but every girl shall be allowed to live." *(Ex. 1:22)*

וְאֶת עֲמָלֵנוּ: אֵלוּ הַבָּנִים, כְּמָה שֶׁנֶּאֱמַר: כָּל הַבֵּן הַיִּלּוֹד הַיְאֹרָה תַּשְׁלִיכֻהוּ, וְכָל הַבַּת תְּחַיּוּן.

Shifra and Puah, two respected Hebrew midwives, were credited as the first resistors against Pharaoh. They refused to obey Pharaoh's command to kill the male Hebrew babies whose birthings they attended.[16]

When the Pharaoh threatened the midwives with death by fire, they outwardly agreed to his plan. Shifra and Puah returned to their people and helped the Israelite women hide their sons and nurture their babies to insure the survival of the Jewish people. When Pharaoh questioned what happened to the male Hebrew babies, the midwives said that the Hebrew women "are not like Egyptian women; for they are robust and give birth before the midwives arrive." *(Ex. 1:19)* The actions of the midwives gave the people courage to withstand their oppression and the vision for how to overcome it.[17]

When Amram, the spiritual leader of the Israelites, heard Pharaoh's decree calling for the death of all male children, he divorced his wife, Yocheved, to avoid having children. Many Hebrews followed his example.

After a time, Amram's daughter, Miriam, prophesied, "Another son shall be born to my parents; he shall free Israel from bondage and deliver them out of the hands of the Egyptians." She reproved her father, telling him that his decision was even crueler than the Pharaoh's decree.[18] "Pharaoh plans the destruction of the male children, while you decree the destruction of all children—female and male. It is unlikely that Pharaoh's decree will succeed, because he is wicked and unjust; but yours is likely to be upheld, because you are so pious and good."[19]

Soon afterward, Yocheved gave birth to Moses. The importance of bearing children cannot be underestimated. It was the greatest indication of the Israelites' faith in the future and in a better world.[20]

Our Sages said: "By virtue of the righteous women of that generation, the Israelites were redeemed from Egypt."

Moses was saved by three women. His mother hid him in a basket among the bulrushes of the river Nile and later nursed him; Bethiah, the Pharaoh's daughter, drew Moses from his hiding place and adopted him; his sister, Miriam, watched over him and later suggested her mother, Yocheved, as a wet nurse.[21] Thus did Miriam assure her brother's safe upbringing in the arms of his real mother in the palace of the Pharaoh.[22]

Pharaoh's daughter named the baby Moses, saying, "I drew him forth from the water."

וְאֶת לַחֲצֵנוּ
"And our oppression." *(Deut. 26:7)*

This refers to the severity used to crush our spirit. And it is written: "Moreover, I have seen how the Egyptians oppress them." *(Ex. 3:9)*

וְאֶת לַחֲצֵנוּ: זוֹ הַדְּחַק, כְּמָה שֶׁנֶּאֱמַר, וְגַם רָאִיתִי אֶת הַלַּחַץ, אֲשֶׁר מִצְרַיִם לֹחֲצִים אֹתָם.

Moses grew up in the palace as an Egyptian prince, but he was drawn to his people and his roots. One day he saw an Egyptian beating an Israelite. His anger could not be contained. He killed the Egyptian and later fled to Midian,[23] fearing the Pharaoh. He married Zipporah, daughter of Jethro, a Midian priest. Moses became a shepherd to Jethro's flock.

But Moses' destiny followed him to the desert. One day, while rescuing a lost lamb, he had a vision of a burning, but unconsumed, bush. Then God spoke from out of the bush: "Do not despair! Know that I am with your people, and just as the bush seems to burn, yet is not consumed, so Israel, though it suffer, will not be destroyed by the Egyptians." Moses returned to Egypt and enlisted the help of his brother, Aaron, and his sister, Miriam.

At first, Moses impressed the Jewish leadership. The elders appointed him to ask Pharaoh to let the people go on a three-day religious festival in the desert. Pharaoh refused and the Hebrew slaves went on strike. Pharaoh denounced Moses and Aaron and ordered the taskmasters to deny the slaves straw to make bricks. Pharaoh thus acted like the classic oppressor by tightening, rather than loosening, the bonds of oppression at the first sign of insubordination. The Jewish leadership turned against Moses and Aaron in the classic pattern of oppressed people, who often turn against each other instead of uniting against the oppressor.[24]

Directions: Sing "Someone's in the palace," to the melody of "Someone's in the kitchen with Dinah."

Someone's in the palace with Pharaoh,
Someone's in the palace we know -o-o-o.
Someone's in the palace with Pharaoh,
And we know his name is Mo - ses.

"And God knew . . ."
When the Israelites had grown accustomed to their tasks and began to labor without complaint, then God knew it was time that they be liberated; for the worst slavery is when we learn to endure it. As long as there was no prospect of freedom, the Israelites would not awaken to the bitterness of bondage. First, Moses had to teach the taste of freedom's hope, and only then did servitude taste bitter. So though bitter slavery is first, and then comes liberation, the Seder teaches us to taste the ***matzah* of freedom** first, and only then to taste the bitter herbs of bondage.

Herbert Bronstein (adapted)

וַיּוֹצִאֵנוּ יְיָ מִמִּצְרַיִם
"Then God brought us out of Egypt"

This stresses one basic truth. God, alone, led us out of Egypt! As it is written: "God brought us out of Egypt": not by an angel, not by a seraph,* and not by a messenger. It was You alone in Your glory, and by Yourself. As it is written, "On that night I will pass through the land of Egypt, and I will strike down every firstborn of Egypt, from man to beast. I will execute judgments against all the gods of Egypt; I am the Eternal." *(Ex. 12:12)*

"And I will pass through the land of Egypt"—I and not an angel! "And I will strike down all the firstborn of Egypt"—I and not a seraph! "I will judge all the gods of Egypt"—I and not a messenger! "I am the Eternal"—I and none other!

וַיּוֹצִאֵנוּ יְיָ מִמִּצְרַיִם: לֹא עַל יְדֵי מַלְאָךְ, וְלֹא עַל יְדֵי שָׂרָף, וְלֹא עַל יְדֵי שָׁלִיחַ. אֶלָּא הַקָּדוֹשׁ בָּרוּךְ הוּא בִּכְבוֹדוֹ וּבְעַצְמוֹ. שֶׁנֶּאֱמַר, וְעָבַרְתִּי בְאֶרֶץ מִצְרַיִם בַּלַּיְלָה הַזֶּה, וְהִכֵּיתִי כָל בְּכוֹר בְּאֶרֶץ מִצְרַיִם מֵאָדָם וְעַד בְּהֵמָה, וּבְכָל אֱלֹהֵי מִצְרַיִם אֶעֱשֶׂה שְׁפָטִים, אֲנִי יְיָ:

וְעָבַרְתִּי בְאֶרֶץ מִצְרַיִם בַּלַּיְלָה הַזֶּה, אֲנִי וְלֹא מַלְאָךְ. וְהִכֵּיתִי כָל בְּכוֹר בְּאֶרֶץ מִצְרַיִם. אֲנִי וְלֹא שָׂרָף. אֲנִי וְלֹא הַשָּׁלִיחַ. אֲנִי יְיָ, אֲנִי הוּא וּבְכָל אֱלֹהֵי מִצְרַיִם אֶעֱשֶׂה שְׁפָטִים, וְלֹא אַחֵר.

---

*This refers to the archangel, Gabriel, who is called a seraph, literally meaning "a flaming creation."

Moses received the Torah on Sinai and taught it to the children of Israel. Thus, the Torah is known as "The Five Books of Moses." But the burial place of Moses was never revealed in the Torah, so that his tomb can never become an object of worship. For this same reason, Moses' name does not appear in the Haggadah unless it is a part of a quotation or a prayer. For God, alone, is the Hero of the Exodus.25

בְּיָד חֲזָקָה.
"With a mighty hand."

This refers to the cattle plague. As it is written, "Behold the hand of the Eternal will strike down your cattle in the field, your horses, donkeys, camels, oxen and sheep with a deadly plague."*(Ex. 9:3)*

בְּיָד חֲזָקָה: זוֹ הַדֶּבֶר. כְּמָה שֶׁנֶּאֱמַר, הִנֵּה יַד יְיָ הוֹיָה בְּמִקְנְךָ אֲשֶׁר בַּשָּׂדֶה, בַּסּוּסִים בַּחֲמֹרִים בַּגְּמַלִּים, בַּבָּקָר וּבַצֹּאן, דֶּבֶר כָּבֵד מְאֹד.

This is the fifth of the plagues God brought upon the Egyptians.

וּבִזְרֹעַ נְטוּיָה
"With an outstretched arm."

This is the sword, as it is written, "A drawn sword was in God's hand outstretched over Jerusalem."*(I Chronicles 12:16)*

וּבִזְרֹעַ נְטוּיָה: זוֹ הַחֶרֶב, כְּמָה שֶׁנֶּאֱמַר, וְחַרְבּוֹ שְׁלוּפָה בְּיָדוֹ, נְטוּיָה עַל יְרוּשָׁלָיִם.

This refers to the tenth plague God brought upon the Egyptians with the slaying of the firstborn.

Commentators tell us that when the Egyptian firstborn heard of their impending fate, they took up arms to force the government to free the Jews in order to save themselves. Intense fighting took place between child and parent.26 Many lives were lost in this battle because the Egyptians chose to sacrifice the lives of their children rather than give freedom to the Jews.

וּבְמוֹרָא גָּדוֹל
"With awesome power."

This refers to the Revelation of the Divine Presence. As it is written, "Has any god ever sought to go and to take one nation from the very midst of another nation through trials, signs, wonders and war, and with a mighty hand, and an outstretched arm, and with awesome power, according to all that the Eternal your God did for you in Egypt before your very eyes?" *(Deut. 4:34)*

וּבְמוֹרָא גָּדוֹל: זֶה גִּלּוּי שְׁכִינָה, כְּמָה שֶׁנֶּאֱמַר, אוֹ הֲנִסָּה אֱלֹהִים לָבוֹא לָקַחַת לוֹ גוֹי מִקֶּרֶב גּוֹי, בְּמַסֹּת בְּאֹתֹת וּבְמוֹפְתִים, וּבְמִלְחָמָה, וּבְיָד חֲזָקָה, וּבִזְרוֹעַ נְטוּיָה, וּבְמוֹרָאִים גְּדֹלִים, כְּכֹל אֲשֶׁר עָשָׂה לָכֶם יְיָ אֱלֹהֵיכֶם בְּמִצְרַיִם, לְעֵינֶיךָ.

וּבְאֹתוֹת
"With signs"

This refers to the rod of Moses, as it is written, "Take this rod in your hand, and with it perform the signs." *(Ex. 4:17)*

וּבְאֹתוֹת: זֶה הַמַּטֶּה, כְּמָה שֶׁנֶּאֱמַר, וְאֶת הַמַּטֶּה הַזֶּה תִּקַּח בְּיָדֶךָ, אֲשֶׁר תַּעֲשֶׂה בּוֹ אֶת הָאֹתֹת.

וּבְמֹפְתִים
"And wonders." *(Deut. 26:8)*

This refers to the first plague of blood. As it is written, "I will show wonders in the heavens and on the earth."

וּבְמֹפְתִים: זֶה הַדָּם, כְּמָה שֶׁנֶּאֱמַר, וְנָתַתִּי מוֹפְתִים בַּשָּׁמַיִם וּבָאָרֶץ.

"When, at God's command, Moses instructed Aaron to raise his staff and strike the water of the Nile, all the waters in Egypt turned into blood." *(Ex. 7:19)* The Nile is an artery of the whole of Egypt, where rainfall is rare. The overflow of the Nile, and its flooding of the whole country, amply replaces the lack of natural rainfall. Therefore, the ancient Egyptians worshipped the Nile and the crocodile that inhabits it as idols. When the Nile was turned into a river of blood, and all its animal life killed, the object of Egypt's idolatrous worship became repugnant to them. The bloody waters of the Nile taught the Egyptians about the existence of a power that they could not fight.[27]

Directions: Dip a small spoon or the second finger of your hand into your wine cup and spill out some wine as the following three words are mentioned:

1.	Dam	Blood
2.	Va-esh	Fire
3.	V'tim'rot ashan	**Pillars of Smoke** *(Joel 3:3)*

דָּם,
וָאֵשׁ
וְתִימְרוֹת עָשָׁן

Another explanation is: "With a mighty hand" indicates two plagues; "With an outstretched arm," another two; "With great awe," another two; "With signs," two more; "And with wonders," another two thus making the ten plagues.

דָּבָר אַחֵר: בְּיָד חֲזָקָה שְׁתַּיִם. וּבִזְרֹעַ נְטוּיָה שְׁתַּיִם. וּבְמוֹרָא גָּדוֹל שְׁתַּיִם. וּבְאֹתוֹת שְׁתַּיִם. וּבְמֹפְתִים שְׁתַּיִם.

Nothing Moses or Aaron did or said made a lasting impact on Pharaoh. He was unmoved by pleas for justice and mercy[28] and scornful of those humble spokesmen for a mass of slaves.

Directions: Sing "Every time bad things..." sung to the melody of "Clementine."

Every time bad things got started,	But as soon as things got better,
He would almost let them go.	He would switch and tell them "No!"

With each plague, Pharaoh became more defiant. But the tenth plague finally broke his will; every Egyptian firstborn son, including the Pharaoh's, was slain. The Pharaoh hastily relented and told Moses to hurry the Israelites out of the land. Miriam, the prophet, organized the women to take charge of all the details of the departure from Egypt.[29]

The ten plagues mark the climax of Israel's liberation from a decadent civilization in which they had lived for 210 years. On that day, Israel went forth into freedom, 600,000 strong, God's Presence going before them.

But Pharaoh had a change of heart as soon as conditions returned to normal. He dispatched his troops to recapture the fleeing slaves, who were now by the shores of the Red Sea. Israel stood uncertain: before them–the sea, behind them–Egypt's army. The Israelites were frightened and, in their panic, turned on Moses for bringing this danger upon them.[30]

The waters divided only after Nachshon ben Amminadav, chief of the tribe of Judah, walked into the sea. By doing this, he acted as a free human being who was ready to take the ultimate risk for freedom.[31] After the Jews followed Nachshon crossing over in safety, the waters immediately turned back and covered all of Pharaoh's army, horses, and chariots.

Moses and the Children of Israel sang a song of praise to God. Miriam led the women in song and dance, chanting, "Sing to God, for the Eternal is highly exalted; God has hurled both horse and rider into the sea." *(Ex. 15:20-21)*

Our Joy Is Less Than Full

A full cup is the symbol of complete joy. But though we celebrate the triumph of Israel's freedom, our happiness is not complete knowing that our redemption caused suffering to others. For as Abraham Joshua Heschel once said, "In a free society, some are guilty; all are responsible."

As we mention plague after plague brought upon the Egyptians, we spill some wine from our cup of gladness to express our sorrow over the losses that each plague exacted. Our cup of joy is less than full when any human being, even our enemy, suffers.

The *Midrash* relates that when the Egyptians were drowned in the Red Sea and the angels wanted to sing *Halleluyah*, God rebuked them: "How can you sing *Halleluyah* when My children are drowning?" *(Megillah 10b)* That is why only half *Hallel*, and not the full *Hallel*, is recited during the last six days of Passover.

Rabbi Yaakov Culi (1689-1732) was the initiator of an important series of Ladino Torah commentaries called Me'am Lo'ez. He said the first group of plagues—flood, frogs and lice—was intended to demonstrate the existence of God, which Pharaoh had denied. And God said, "With this you will know that I am God." *(Ex. 7:17)* The second group of plagues—beasts, cattle disease and boils—was meant to indicate that God oversees the lower world as well as the upper spheres. God said these plagues were coming "So that you may know that I am God right here on earth." *(Ex. 8:18)* The third and final group of plagues came to demonstrate that God is unique among all the powers in the universe, which Pharaoh refused to accept. God said the last plagues were coming "So that you may know that there is none like Me in all the earth." *(Ex. 9:14)*

Directions: Spill a drop of wine/grape juice into your saucer with a spoon or the second finger of your hand, as each plague is mentioned. Using the finger symbolically recalls that "the finger of God" brought on the plagues. **Pass out Plague Bags to guests.** *Do not open bags yet.*

E-lu e-ser ma-kot she-hevi ha-ka-dosh ba-ruch hu al hamitz'rim b'mitz'ra-yim, v'elu hen:	אֵלּוּ עֶשֶׂר מַכּוֹת שֶׁהֵבִיא הַקָּדוֹשׁ בָּרוּךְ הוּא עַל הַמִּצְרִים בְּמִצְרַיִם, וְאֵלּוּ הֵן:

These are the ten plagues which the Holy One, Blessed are You, brought upon the Egyptians in Egypt:

1.	Blood	Dam	דָּם.
2.	Frogs	Tz'far'de-a	צְפַרְדֵּעַ.
3.	Lice	Kinim	כִּנִּים.
4.	Wild Beasts	Arov	עָרוֹב.
5.	Cattle Disease	Dever	דֶּבֶר.
6.	Boils	Sh'chin	שְׁחִין.
7.	Hail	Barad	בָּרָד.

8.	Locusts	Ar'beh	אַרְבֶּה.
9.	Darkness	Cho-shech	חֹשֶׁךְ.
10.	Death of Firstborn	Makat B'cho-rot	מַכַּת בְּכוֹרוֹת.

Directions: Leader recites the number and the plague in English and Hebrew. Then each guest spills a drop of wine/grape juice into his/her saucer. The guest with that numbered plague bag opens the bag and spills the contents onto the table. You may then sing the related stanza.

Sing **The Ten Plagues** (*Sung to "She'll Be Comin' Round the Mountain"*)

Bad things will come to Egypt, don't you know (Repeat)
Bad things will come to Egypt (Repeat)
Bad things will come to Egypt 'til we go!

Author unknown.

1. Blood   Dam (Dip; open bag; sing stanza.)
First God will change the Nile into blood (**ick, ick**) (Repeat)
There'll be nothing left to drink
So you won't feel in the pink
When God changes the water into blood. (**ick, ick**)

2. Frogs   Tz-far-dei-a (Dip; open bag; sing stanza.)
Slimy frogs will be all over everything (**ribbit, ribbit**) (Repeat)
They will jump all over you-ou
They will jump into your stew-ew
Slimy frogs will be all over everything (**ribbit, ribbitt**)

3. Lice   Kin'im (Dip; open bag; sing stanza.)
Lice will make your bodies itch and itch and itch (**scratch, scratch**) (Repeat)
The heads of poor and rich,
Even animals will itch
When lice will make your bodies itch and itch. (**scratch, scratch**)

4. Wild Animals   Arov (Dip; open bag; sing stanza.)
Wild animals will scare you all to death (**roar, roar**) (Repeat)
You'll be frightened of their roars
As they threaten at your doors
Wild animals will scare you all to death (**roar, roar**)

5. Cattle Disease   De'ver (Dip; open bag; sing stanza.)
Your cattle will get sick and die like flies (**no moos**) (Repeat)
No milk will fill your cu-up
And no meat there'll be to su-up
When your cattle all get sick and die like flies (**no moos**)

6. Boils   Sh'chin (Dip; open bag; sing stanza.)
Your skin will get big sores all over it (**oy, oy**) (Repeat)
You will cry because they hurt you.
No medicine will cure you.
And you'll even get sores down where you-ou sit! (**oy, oy**)

7. Hail   Barad (Dip; open bag; sing stanza.)
Icy hail will fall upon you from the sky (**knock, knock**) (Repeat)
You may try to hide your he-ad
You may crawl beneath your be-ed
But all the outside plants will surely die. (**knock, knock**)

8. Locusts   Ar'beh (Dip; open bag; sing stanza.)
The locusts they will swarm around your land (**buzz, buzz**) (Repeat)
They will eat all plants of gree-een
No broccoli will be see-een
When the locusts they will swarm around your land. (**buzz, buzz**)

9. Darkness   Cho'shech (Dip; open bag; sing stanza.)
The day will turn as dark as night can be (**oh, oh**) (Repeat)
You won't see your family's faces
Or old familiar places
When the day turns dark as night could ever be. (**oh, oh**)

10. Death of the First Born   Makat B'cho-rot (Dip; open bag; sing stanza.)
God will give you one last chance to let us go. (**LET US GO**) (Repeat)
As midnight passes by-y
All your first born sons will die-ie
And your people will cry out if we can't go. (**WE'D BETTER GO**)

We spill **three** more drops of wine, one each to represent our **past, present, and future contributions to Jewish continuance.**

Directions: To help remember the order of the ten plagues as they occurred, Rabbi Judah put together the first Hebrew letter of each plague and formed three words. As each of the three words is mentioned, spill some wine from your cup.

Rabbi Judah used to refer to these ten plagues as follows:

רַבִּי יְהוּדָה הָיָה נוֹתֵן בָּהֶם סִמָּנִים:

D'TZACH, A-DASH B'ACHAV.

דְּצַ"ךְ עֲדַ"שׁ בְּאַחַ"ב

Freedom from a master is not the end of a liberation struggle, but only the beginning. During the years of bondage, the Jews saw themselves as victims—weak, and powerless. So although they had wrenched their bodies free of bondage, their spirits were still enslaved. They were unsure of their identity, incapable of trusting themselves or each other, fearful of risks and responsibilities. They did not even trust their own chosen leaders. Many times they regretted bitterly having given up the security of slavery for the insecurity and dangers of freedom.

They did not go back to slavery in Egypt. But neither could they go forward to self-determination in the Promised Land. The entire generation of slaves, except for two men, wandered in the desert for forty years.

But the next generation, born to the precarious life in the desert and free of the values and painful memories of Egyptian slavery, were independent in both body and soul. They went up to the Promised Land.

Aviva Cantor (Excerpted from The Egalitarian Hagada © 2000)

Da-yenu דַּיֵּנוּ

Da-yenu builds into an intensity of praise and thanksgiving to God for the fifteen Divine Favors, starting with our Exodus from Egypt to the building of the Holy Temple. *Da-yenu* has been translated as "thank you" and "it would have been enough."

Kamah ma-alot tovot lamakom Aleinu!

כַּמָה מַעֲלוֹת טוֹבוֹת לַמָּקוֹם עָלֵינוּ:

How thankful we are for the many good deeds God showered upon us!

Ilu hotzi-anu mi-mitz'rayim v'lo asa vahem sh'fatim, *DA-YENU.**

אִלּוּ הוֹצִיאָנוּ מִמִּצְרַיִם, וְלֹא עָשָׂה בָהֶם שְׁפָטִים, דַּיֵּנוּ:*

Had God brought us out from Egypt and not judged against its people, *DA-YENU.**

Ilu asa vahem sh'fatim v'lo asa velo-heihem, *DA-YENU.**

אִלּוּ עָשָׂה בָהֶם שְׁפָטִים, וְלֹא עָשָׂה בֵאלֹהֵיהֶם, דַּיֵּנוּ:*

Had God judged against its people and not destroyed their idols, *DA-YENU.**

Ilu asa velo-heihem v'lo harag et b'cho-reihem, *DA-YENU.**

אִלּוּ עָשָׂה בֵאלֹהֵיהֶם, וְלֹא הָרַג אֶת בְּכוֹרֵיהֶם, דַּיֵּנוּ:*

Had God destroyed their idols and not slain their firstborn, *DA-YENU.**

Ilu harag et b'cho-reihem v'lo natan lanu et mamonam, *DA-YENU.**

אִלּוּ הָרַג אֶת בְּכוֹרֵיהֶם, וְלֹא נָתַן לָנוּ אֶת מָמוֹנָם, דַּיֵּנוּ:*

Had God slain their firstborn and not given us their wealth, *DA-YENU.**

Ilu natan lanu et mamonam v'lo kara lanu et ha-yam, *DA-YENU.**

אִלּוּ נָתַן לָנוּ אֶת מָמוֹנָם, וְלֹא קָרַע לָנוּ אֶת הַיָּם, דַּיֵּנוּ:*

Had God given us their wealth and not divided the Sea for us, *DA-YENU.**

***Chorus:** Da-da-yenu (3 times), da-yenu, da-yenu, da-yenu, da-da-yenu (3 times) da-yenu, da-yenu.

Ilu kara lanu et ha-yam v'lo he-e-viranu
V'tocho becharavah, *DA-YENU.**

אִלּוּ קָרַע לָנוּ אֶת הַיָּם,
וְלֹא הֶעֱבִירָנוּ בְּתוֹכוֹ בֶּחָרָבָה,
דַּיֵּנוּ:*

    Had God divided the Sea for us and not brought us through dry land, *DA-YENU.**

Ilu he-e-viranu v'tocho becharavah v'lo
shika tza-reinu b'tocho, *DA-YENU.**

אִלּוּ הֶעֱבִירָנוּ בְּתוֹכוֹ
בֶּחָרָבָה וְלֹא שִׁקַּע צָרֵינוּ
בְּתוֹכוֹ,
דַּיֵּנוּ:*

    Had God brought us through dry land and not drowned our oppressors in it, *DA-YENU.**

Ilu shika tza-reinu b'tocho v'lo sipek
tzar'kenu bamid'bar ar'ba-im shanah,
DA-YENU.*

אִלּוּ שִׁקַּע צָרֵינוּ בְּתוֹכוֹ,
וְלֹא סִפֵּק צָרְכֵּנוּ בַּמִּדְבָּר
אַרְבָּעִים שָׁנָה,
דַּיֵּנוּ:*

    Had God drowned our oppressors in it and not sustained us for forty years in the desert, *DA-YENU.**

Ilu sipek tzar'kenu bamid'bar ar'ba-im
shanah v'lo he-e-chilanu et haman,
DA-YENU.*

אִלּוּ סִפֵּק צָרְכֵּנוּ בַּמִּדְבָּר
אַרְבָּעִים שָׁנָה,
וְלֹא הֶאֱכִילָנוּ אֶת הַמָּן,
דַּיֵּנוּ:*

    Had God sustained us for forty years in the desert and not fed us with manna, *DA-YENU.**

Ilu he-e-chilanu et haman v'lo natan lanu
et HaShabbat, *DA-YENU.**

אִלּוּ הֶאֱכִילָנוּ אֶת הַמָּן,
וְלֹא נָתַן לָנוּ אֶת הַשַּׁבָּת,
דַּיֵּנוּ:*

    Had God fed us with manna, and not given us the Sabbath, *DA-YENU.*

Ilu natan lanu et HaShabbat v'lo ker'vanu
lif'nei Har Sinai, *DA-YENU.**

אִלּוּ נָתַן לָנוּ אֶת הַשַּׁבָּת,
וְלֹא קֵרְבָנוּ לִפְנֵי הַר סִינַי,
דַּיֵּנוּ:*

    Had God given us the Sabbath and not brought us to Mount Sinai, *DA-YENU.**

Ilu ker'vanu lif'nei Har Sinai v'lo natan lanu et Hatorah, *DA-YENU.**

אִלּוּ קֵרְבָנוּ לִפְנֵי הַר סִינַי,
וְלֹא נָתַן לָנוּ אֶת הַתּוֹרָה,
דַּיֵּנוּ:*

    Had God brought us to Mount Sinai and not given us the Torah, *DA-YENU.**

Ilu natan lanu et Hatorah v'lo hich'nisanu l'eretz Yis'ra-el, *DA-YENU.**

אִלּוּ נָתַן לָנוּ אֶת הַתּוֹרָה,
וְלֹא הִכְנִיסָנוּ לְאֶרֶץ יִשְׂרָאֵל,
דַּיֵּנוּ:*

    Had God given us the Torah and not brought us into the Land of Israel, *DA-YENU.**

Ilu hich'nisanu l'eretz Yis'ra-el v'lo vana lanu et beit Hab'chira, *DA-YENU.**

אִלּוּ הִכְנִיסָנוּ לְאֶרֶץ יִשְׂרָאֵל,
וְלֹא בָנָה לָנוּ אֶת בֵּית הַבְּחִירָה,
דַּיֵּנוּ:*

    Had God brought us into the Land of Israel and not built the Holy Temple for us, *DA-YENU.**

*Chorus: Da-da-yenu (3 times), da-yenu, da-yenu, da-yenu, da-da-yenu (3 times) da-yenu, da-yenu.

How much greater than great are the benefits which God showered upon us in double and redoubled measure! For God brought us out of Egypt **and** judged against its people, **and** destroyed their idols, **and** slew their firstborn, **and** gave us their wealth, **and** divided the Sea for us, **and** brought us through on dry land, **and** drowned our oppressors in it, **and** sustained us in the wilderness for forty years, **and** fed us manna, **and** gave us the Sabbath, **and** brought us to Mount Sinai, **and** gave us the Torah, **and** brought us to the Land of Israel, **and** built the Holy Temple, to atone for all our sins.

עַל אַחַת כַּמָּה וְכַמָּה, טוֹבָה כְפוּלָה וּמְכֻפֶּלֶת לַמָּקוֹם עָלֵינוּ. שֶׁהוֹצִיאָנוּ מִמִּצְרַיִם, וְעָשָׂה בָהֶם שְׁפָטִים, וְעָשָׂה בֵאלֹהֵיהֶם, וְהָרַג אֶת בְּכוֹרֵיהֶם, וְנָתַן לָנוּ אֶת מָמוֹנָם, וְקָרַע לָנוּ אֶת הַיָּם, וְהֶעֱבִירָנוּ בְּתוֹכוֹ בֶּחָרָבָה, וְשִׁקַּע צָרֵינוּ בְּתוֹכוֹ, וְסִפֵּק צָרְכֵּנוּ בַּמִּדְבָּר אַרְבָּעִים שָׁנָה, וְהֶאֱכִילָנוּ אֶת הַמָּן, וְנָתַן לָנוּ אֶת הַשַּׁבָּת, וְקֵרְבָנוּ לִפְנֵי הַר סִינַי, וְנָתַן לָנוּ אֶת הַתּוֹרָה, וְהִכְנִיסָנוּ לְאֶרֶץ יִשְׂרָאֵל, וּבָנָה לָנוּ אֶת בֵּית הַבְּחִירָה, לְכַפֵּר עַל כָּל עֲוֹנוֹתֵינוּ.

The Three Symbols of Passover פֶּסַח מַצָּה וּמָרוֹר:

There are many interesting and important symbols at the Passover Seder, but three among these are so significant that

Rabban Gamli-el used to say: "Those who do not explain the following three symbols at the Seder on Passover have not fulfilled their duty"

רַבָּן גַּמְלִיאֵל הָיָה אוֹמֵר: כָּל שֶׁלֹּא אָמַר שְׁלֹשָׁה דְבָרִים אֵלּוּ בַּפֶּסַח, לֹא יָצָא יְדֵי חוֹבָתוֹ, וְאֵלּוּ הֵן:

Pesach, the Passover (Paschal) Lamb;

פֶּסַח,

Matzah, the Unleavened Bread;

מַצָּה,

Maror, the Bitter Herb.

וּמָרוֹר.

Directions: The leader(s) points to the shank bone without touching or lifting it, and asks:

Why did our ancestors eat the **Passover Offering** long ago when the Temple in Jerusalem existed?

פֶּסַח שֶׁהָיוּ אֲבוֹתֵינוּ אוֹכְלִים בִּזְמַן שֶׁבֵּית הַמִּקְדָּשׁ הָיָה קַיָּם, עַל שׁוּם מָה?

It is to remind us that God **passed over** the houses of our ancestors in Egypt and struck the firstborn sons of the Egyptians. As it is written in the Torah, "You shall say that it is a Passover offering, for the Eternal passed over the houses of the children of Israel in Egypt, when striking the Egyptians, but spared our houses; and the people bowed their heads and worshipped." *(Ex. 12:27)*

עַל שׁוּם שֶׁפָּסַח הַקָּדוֹשׁ בָּרוּךְ הוּא עַל בָּתֵּי אֲבוֹתֵינוּ בְּמִצְרַיִם. שֶׁנֶּאֱמַר, וַאֲמַרְתֶּם זֶבַח פֶּסַח הוּא לַייָ, אֲשֶׁר פָּסַח עַל בָּתֵּי בְנֵי יִשְׂרָאֵל בְּמִצְרַיִם, בְּנָגְפּוֹ אֶת מִצְרַיִם, וְאֶת בָּתֵּינוּ הִצִּיל, וַיִּקֹּד הָעָם וַיִּשְׁתַּחֲווּ.

The Israelites' firstborn also deserved to die, for they had assimilated and defiled themselves[32] by paying homage to the lamb, which was worshipped by the Egyptians. However, God had mercy on them and instructed each household to sacrifice the very animal revered by the Egyptians as a god. By doing so, the Israelites rejected animal worship and proved their love of God and courage in the face of the enemy. As a result, God found them worthy of redemption and passed over the homes of the Israelites, striking only at the Egyptians.

The Passover sacrifice (*Korban Pesach*) has given its name to our whole festival. God commanded our ancestors to sacrifice the Passover Lamb on the tenth day of *Nisan*, a Sabbath now known as the *Sabbath Hagadol*, the Great Sabbath.

Directions: The leader(s) raises the middle Matzah and asks:

Matzah: What is the meaning of the *Matzah* that we eat?

מַצָּה זוּ שֶׁאָנוּ אוֹכְלִים, עַל שׁוּם מָה?

The *Matzah* is to remind us that the dough of our ancestors did not have time to rise before God appeared and redeemed them. As the Torah states: "They baked the dough which they brought out from Egypt into unleavened cakes, because it did not rise. They were driven out of Egypt and could not linger, nor had they prepared any food for themselves." *(Ex. 12:34)*

עַל שׁוּם שֶׁלֹּא הִסְפִּיק בְּצֵקָם שֶׁל אֲבוֹתֵינוּ לְהַחֲמִיץ, עַד שֶׁנִּגְלָה עֲלֵיהֶם מֶלֶךְ מַלְכֵי הַמְּלָכִים הַקָּדוֹשׁ בָּרוּךְ הוּא וּגְאָלָם. שֶׁנֶּאֱמַר, וַיֹּאפוּ אֶת הַבָּצֵק, אֲשֶׁר הוֹצִיאוּ מִמִּצְרַיִם, עֻגֹת מַצּוֹת כִּי לֹא חָמֵץ. כִּי גֹרְשׁוּ מִמִּצְרַיִם, וְלֹא יָכְלוּ לְהִתְמַהְמֵהַּ, וְגַם צֵדָה לֹא עָשׂוּ לָהֶם.

The meaning of *Matzah* is threefold. *Matzah* represents the bread of poverty that our ancestors ate as slaves in the land of Egypt. Eating the heavy and tasteless wafer reminds us that as humble slaves we were denied all human comforts and pleasures. *Matzah* also reminds us of the hasty flight of the Israelites from Egypt when God redeemed them. A third meaning of *Matzah* is the bread of freedom our ancestors ate when the hour of freedom arrived.[33]

Directions: The leader raises the Maror and asks:

Maror: What is the meaning of the **Bitter Herbs**, which we eat?

מָרוֹר זֶה שֶׁאָנוּ אוֹכְלִים, עַל שׁוּם מָה?

We eat the *Maror*, or Bitter Herbs, because the Egyptians embittered the lives of our ancestors in Egypt; as the Torah says: "They made their lives bitter with hard labor in mortar and brick, and with every kind of work in the field. All the labor which the Egyptians forced upon them was harsh." (Ex. 1:14)

עַל שׁוּם שֶׁמֵּרְרוּ הַמִּצְרִים אֶת חַיֵּי אֲבוֹתֵינוּ בְּמִצְרַיִם, שֶׁנֶּאֱמַר, וַיְמָרְרוּ אֶת חַיֵּיהֶם בַּעֲבֹדָה קָשָׁה, בְּחֹמֶר וּבִלְבֵנִים, וּבְכָל עֲבֹדָה בַּשָּׂדֶה, אֵת כָּל עֲבֹדָתָם אֲשֶׁר עָבְדוּ בָהֶם בְּפָרֶךְ.

> According to Rabbi Yaacov Culi, there are three words for romaine lettuce in Hebrew: *maror*, *chasa*, and *chazeret*. It is called *maror*, meaning bitter, because the Egyptians embittered our lives in Egypt. At first, romaine is sweet, but becomes bitter when fully mature, as with the Israelites whose lives were sweet until they were degraded into slaves.
>
> Romaine is called *chasa* (mercy-*chas*), because God saw their degradation and had mercy on them. Romaine is also called *chazeret*, to symbolize that the Israelites were so degraded they had to resort to begging (*chazar*) in order to survive.

In the Bible, the Jews were "chosen" for no reason they could understand, and this divine selection was as much a burden as a blessing—a burden they kept trying to throw off or evade by human means. In fact, the Israelites were driven into captivity by the wrath of [God] for defying God's commandments.

This role of "The Chosen People" has been so much misunderstood—willfully or not—by those who assumed it stood for a self-appointed "honor" the Jews took for themselves which conferred a sense of superiority, rather than an obligation they were suffered to bear until the day of redemption.

Ironically, though other peoples have suffered much the same way, history has dictated that only the Jews continued [and still continue] to pay the price.

Sydney J. Harris (adapted from "Chosen People wear yoke not a superiority complex")

In the following verses, the first part stresses that we must personally and individually see ourselves as having been enslaved in Egypt and then redeemed by God. The second part tells us that the purpose of our Exodus was to settle in the Holy Land under God's Rule. Because we chose to

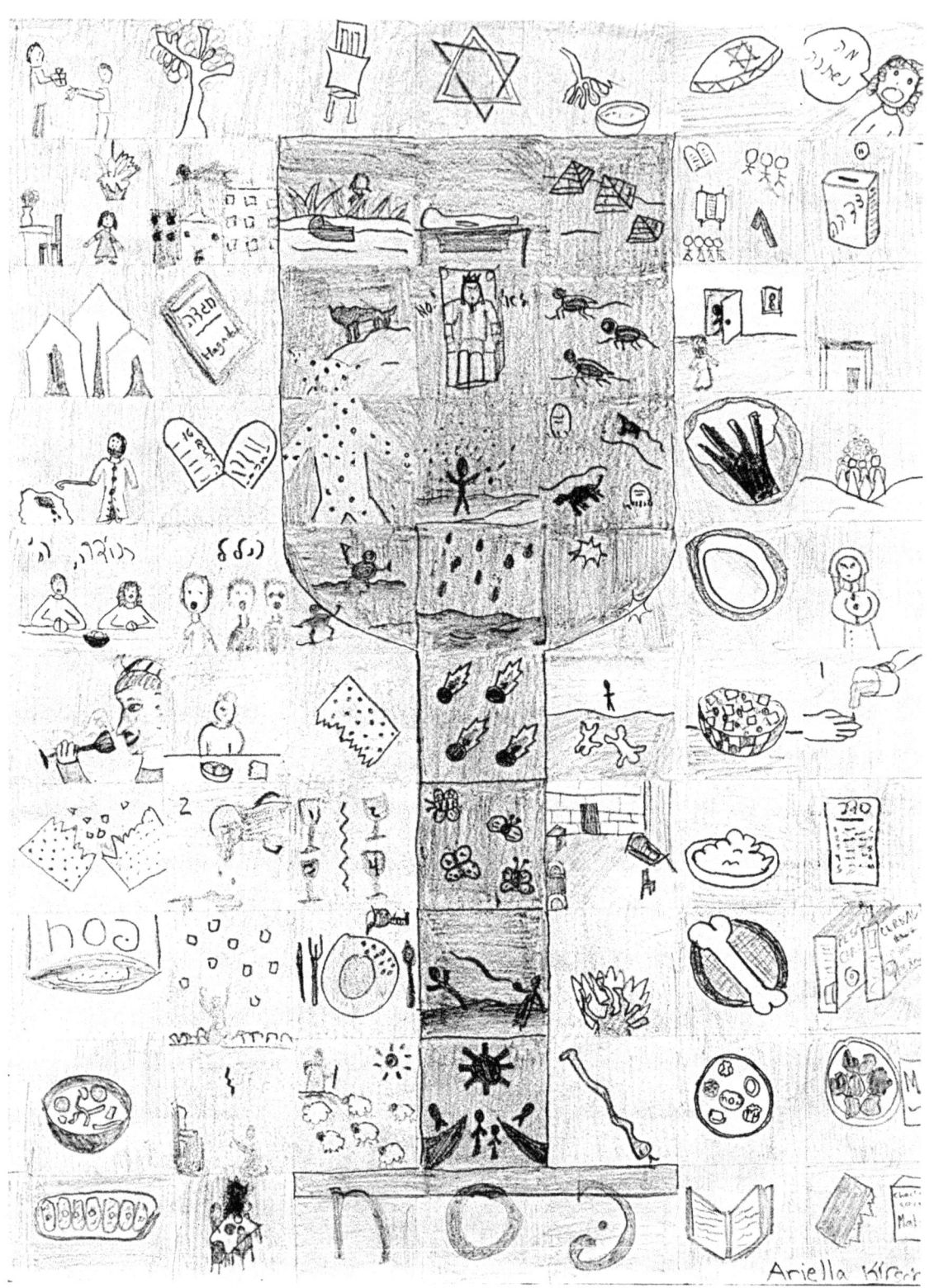

Ariella Kiroc

recognize and acknowledge the Almighty, God chose us to carry out the mission to teach God's ways to the world. "The price Israel pays for Divine Revelation is its responsibility to live up to it."[34]

Directions: Read with great feeling

In every generation, each of us is obligated to feel as though we personally took part in the Exodus from Egypt; as the Torah says: "And you shall tell your child on that day, 'It is because of what God did for me when I came out of Egypt.' " *(Ex. 13:8)* For it is not only our ancestors whom the Holy One, blessed are You, redeemed from slavery, but we were also redeemed with them. As the Torah says: "God brought us out from there so that the Eternal might lead us to and give us the land which God promised to our ancestors." *(Deut. 6:23)*

בְּכָל דּוֹר וָדוֹר חַיָּב אָדָם לִרְאוֹת אֶת עַצְמוֹ כְּאִלּוּ הוּא יָצָא מִמִּצְרַיִם, שֶׁנֶּאֱמַר, וְהִגַּדְתָּ לְבִנְךָ בַּיּוֹם הַהוּא לֵאמֹר, בַּעֲבוּר זֶה עָשָׂה יְיָ לִי, בְּצֵאתִי מִמִּצְרָיִם. לֹא אֶת אֲבוֹתֵינוּ בִּלְבָד גָּאַל הַקָּדוֹשׁ בָּרוּךְ הוּא, אֶלָּא אַף אוֹתָנוּ גָּאַל עִמָּהֶם, שֶׁנֶּאֱמַר, וְאוֹתָנוּ הוֹצִיא מִשָּׁם, לְמַעַן הָבִיא אֹתָנוּ לָתֶת לָנוּ אֶת הָאָרֶץ אֲשֶׁר נִשְׁבַּע לַאֲבֹתֵינוּ.

Directions: Sing B'chol dor vador chayav

B'chol dor vador chayav
Chayav Adam lirot
Lirot, et atz'mo k'e-lu hu

K'e-lu hu yatza Mi-mitz-rayim
She-neh-eh-mar.

Directions: Cover the Matzot, all raise your cup of wine in your right hand and say

Therefore, it is our duty to thank and praise, to be grateful and glorify, to exalt and acclaim, to bless and esteem, and to honor the One Who performed all these miracles for our ancestors and for us. God brought us from slavery to freedom, from sorrow to joy, from mourning to festivity, from darkness to great light, and from bondage to redemption. Let us, therefore, sing a new song before God. Halleluyah!

Praise the Eternal!

לְפִיכָךְ אֲנַחְנוּ חַיָּבִים לְהוֹדוֹת לְהַלֵּל, לְשַׁבֵּחַ, לְפָאֵר, לְרוֹמֵם, לְהַדֵּר, לְבָרֵךְ, לְעַלֵּה, וּלְקַלֵּס, לְמִי שֶׁעָשָׂה לַאֲבוֹתֵינוּ וְלָנוּ אֶת כָּל הַנִּסִּים הָאֵלּוּ. הוֹצִיאָנוּ מֵעַבְדוּת לְחֵרוּת, מִיָּגוֹן לְשִׂמְחָה, וּמֵאֵבֶל לְיוֹם טוֹב, וּמֵאֲפֵלָה לְאוֹר גָּדוֹל, וּמִשִּׁעְבּוּד לִגְאֻלָּה. וְנֹאמַר לְפָנָיו שִׁירָה חֲדָשָׁה. הַלְלוּיָהּ.

Directions: Put down the wine cup and continue.

Psalms of Praise and Thanksgiving   הַלֵּל   Hallel

Hallel is a natural outpouring of gratitude to God. It precedes and follows the festive meal to indicate that the meal is part of the religious service. In Judaism, eating is not merely the consumption of food, but is sanctified with prayer and *Div'rei Torah*, words of the Torah. The first section of the *Hallel* (before the meal) deals specifically with the redemption from Egypt. The second section praises God for the ultimate redemption of the Jewish people and the world.[35]

PSALM 113—*Responsive Reading*

Halleluyah!   הַלְלוּיָהּ.
Praise the Eternal.
Sing praises, O servants of the Eternal,   הַלְלוּ עַבְדֵי יְיָ,
Praise the name of the Eternal.   הַלְלוּ אֶת שֵׁם יְיָ.
    Blessed is the name of the Eternal   יְהִי שֵׁם יְיָ מְבֹרָךְ,
    now and forevermore.   מֵעַתָּה וְעַד עוֹלָם.

       Halleluyah! Hal'lu avdei Adonai. Hal'lu et shem Adonai.
       Y'hi shem Adonai m'vorach. Me-atah v'ad olam.

From the rising of the sun until its setting,   מִמִּזְרַח שֶׁמֶשׁ עַד מְבוֹאוֹ,
Praised is the name of the Eternal.   מְהֻלָּל שֵׁם יְיָ.
Supreme above all nations is the Eternal;   רָם עַל כָּל גּוֹיִם יְיָ,
Whose glory is above the heavens.   עַל הַשָּׁמַיִם כְּבוֹדוֹ.

Who is like the Eternal our God,   מִי כַּייָ אֱלֹהֵינוּ,
Enthroned so high,   הַמַּגְבִּיהִי לָשָׁבֶת.
    Yet Who looks down,   הַמַּשְׁפִּילִי לִרְאוֹת,
    To consider both heaven and earth?   בַּשָּׁמַיִם וּבָאָרֶץ.

Who raises the poor from the dust,   מְקִימִי מֵעָפָר דָּל,
And lifts up the needy from the ash heap,   מֵאַשְׁפֹּת יָרִים אֶבְיוֹן.
    Giving them a place among nobles,   לְהוֹשִׁיבִי עִם נְדִיבִים,
    Among the nobles of Your people,   עִם נְדִיבֵי עַמּוֹ.

Inviting all who are barren,   מוֹשִׁיבִי עֲקֶרֶת הַבַּיִת,
    To become the joyful nurturers of   אֵם הַבָּנִים שְׂמֵחָה.
    children. Halleluyah!   הַלְלוּיָהּ.

PSALM 114 *Responsive Reading*

B'tzet Yis'ra-el mi-Mitz'ra-yim
Beit Ya-akov me-am lo-ez.*
Hai'ta Y'huda l'kad'sho
Yis'ra-el mam'sh'lotav,
Ha-yam ra-a va-yanos
Ha-yar'den yi-sov l'achor. *(Chorus)

He-ha-rim rak'du ch'eilim,
G'va-ot kiv'nei tzon.
Mah l'cha ha-yam ki tanus,
Hayar'den ti-sov l'achor. *(Chorus)

He-harim tir'k'du ch'eilim,
G'va-ot kiv'nei tzon.
Milif'nei adon chu-li a-retz
Milif'nei Elo-ha Ya-a-kov. *(Chorus)
Hahof'chi ha-tzur agam ma-yim
Chalamish l'ma-y'no ma-yim.* (Chorus)

בְּצֵאת יִשְׂרָאֵל מִמִּצְרָיִם,
בֵּית יַעֲקֹב מֵעַם לֹעֵז.*
הָיְתָה יְהוּדָה לְקָדְשׁוֹ,
יִשְׂרָאֵל מַמְשְׁלוֹתָיו.
הַיָּם רָאָה וַיָּנֹס,
הַיַּרְדֵּן יִסֹּב לְאָחוֹר.*
הֶהָרִים רָקְדוּ כְאֵילִים,
גְּבָעוֹת כִּבְנֵי צֹאן.
מַה לְּךָ הַיָּם כִּי תָנוּס,
הַיַּרְדֵּן תִּסֹּב לְאָחוֹר.*
הֶהָרִים תִּרְקְדוּ כְאֵילִים,
גְּבָעוֹת כִּבְנֵי צֹאן.
מִלִּפְנֵי אָדוֹן חוּלִי אָרֶץ,
מִלִּפְנֵי אֱלוֹהַּ יַעֲקֹב.*
הַהֹפְכִי הַצּוּר אֲגַם מָיִם,
חַלָּמִישׁ לְמַעְיְנוֹ מָיִם.*

When Israel went forth from Egypt,
The house of Jacob, Rachel and Leah
from a people of foreign language,
 Judah became God's sanctuary,
 Israel, God's dominion.
The sea saw it, and fled;
The Jordan turned backward.
 The mountains skipped like rams,
 The hills like young lambs.

What ails you, O sea, that you flee?
O Jordan that you turn backward?
 You mountains, that you skip like rams;
 And you hills, like young lambs?

Tremble, O earth, at the presence of the Eternal,
At the presence of the God of Jacob, Rachel and Leah,
 Who turns the rock into a pool of water,
 The flint into a flowing fountain.

Directions: Cover the Matzot, raise the second cup of wine, and say:

Blessed are You, Eternal our God, Ruler of the universe, Who redeemed us, and redeemed our ancestors from Egypt, and brought us to this night on which we eat *Matzah* and *Maror*. Thus may our Eternal God and God of our ancestors bring us to future holidays and festivals in peace, when we may rejoice in the rebuilding of Zion, Your city, and find delight in serving You. There may we partake in the Passover meal and bring the offerings which shall be acceptable to You. We shall thank You with a new song for our freedom and the redemption of our soul. Blessed are You, O Eternal, Who has redeemed Israel.

בָּרוּךְ אַתָּה יְיָ אֱלֹהֵינוּ מֶלֶךְ הָעוֹלָם, אֲשֶׁר גְּאָלָנוּ וְגָאַל אֶת אֲבוֹתֵינוּ מִמִּצְרַיִם, וְהִגִּיעָנוּ הַלַּיְלָה הַזֶּה, לֶאֱכָל בּוֹ מַצָּה וּמָרוֹר. כֵּן, יְיָ אֱלֹהֵינוּ וֵאלֹהֵי אֲבוֹתֵינוּ, יַגִּיעֵנוּ לְמוֹעֲדִים וְלִרְגָלִים אֲחֵרִים הַבָּאִים לִקְרָאתֵנוּ לְשָׁלוֹם, שְׂמֵחִים בְּבִנְיַן עִירֶךָ וְשָׂשִׂים בַּעֲבוֹדָתֶךָ. וְנֹאכַל שָׁם מִן הַזְּבָחִים וּמִן הַפְּסָחִים, אֲשֶׁר יַגִּיעַ דָּמָם עַל קִיר מִזְבַּחֲךָ לְרָצוֹן. וְנוֹדֶה לְךָ שִׁיר חָדָשׁ עַל גְּאֻלָּתֵנוּ, וְעַל פְּדוּת נַפְשֵׁנוּ. בָּרוּךְ אַתָּה יְיָ, גָּאַל יִשְׂרָאֵל.

Directions: After reciting the following blessing, drink from the second cup of wine while reclining to the left and while savoring our Holy deliverance from slavery.

Baruch Ata Adonai Eloheinu Melech Ha-olam borei p'ri hagafen.

בָּרוּךְ אַתָּה יְיָ אֱלֹהֵינוּ מֶלֶךְ הָעוֹלָם, בּוֹרֵא פְּרִי הַגָּפֶן.

Blessed are You, Eternal our God, Ruler of the universe, Who creates the fruit of the vine.

---

6. Rach'tzah רָחְצָה Wash the Hands

Directions: It is customary to remove all rings and wash the hands before the meal. (**This is a good time to hide the Afikoman.**) *Take a cup or pitcher of water and pour it over the right hand two or three times; reverse hands and pour it two or three times over the left, then dry them. After the hands are washed and before a meal, recite the following blessing and remain silent until the Motzi is said:*

Baruch Ata Adonai Eloheinu Melech Ha-olam, asher kid'shanu b'mitz'votav v'tzivanu al n'tilat yadayim.

בָּרוּךְ אַתָּה יְיָ אֱלֹהֵינוּ מֶלֶךְ הָעוֹלָם, אֲשֶׁר קִדְּשָׁנוּ בְּמִצְוֹתָיו, וְצִוָּנוּ עַל נְטִילַת יָדָיִם.

Blessed are You, Eternal our God, Ruler of the universe, Who sanctified us with Your commandments and instructed us to wash our hands.

Directions: Read poem.

Passover

We were freed
We were freed
We were slaves
We were freed

We were freed by the light of the moon
We were freed by the songs of the stars

We were enslaved by the evil in a land
That wasn't ours
Many hours we suffered
Until
We were freed

That's why we eat matza and bitter herbs
To remember
How hard we had it
Escaping,
Taping up the wounds
Of doom.

by Laurie Singer

7. Motzi-Matzah מוֹצִיא מַצָּה Eat the Matzah

Directions: The leader(s) raises the two whole matzot and the broken middle matzah and recites the usual Ha-Motzi (normally said over two whole loaves of bread).

Baruch Ata Adonai, Eloheinu Melech Ha-olam, hamotzi lechem min ha-aretz.

בָּרוּךְ אַתָּה יְיָ אֱלֹהֵינוּ מֶלֶךְ הָעוֹלָם, הַמּוֹצִיא לֶחֶם מִן הָאָרֶץ.

> Blessed are You, Eternal our God, Ruler of the universe, Who brings forth bread from the earth.

Directions: The leader puts the bottom matzah back in place, for later use in the Korech sandwich. Holding the upper whole and broken middle matzah, the leader recites the blessing for the matzah.

Baruch Ata Adonai, Eloheinu Melech Ha-olam, asher kid'shanu b'mitzvotav v'tzivanu al achilat matzah.

בָּרוּךְ אַתָּה יְיָ אֱלֹהֵינוּ מֶלֶךְ הָעוֹלָם, אֲשֶׁר קִדְּשָׁנוּ בְּמִצְוֹתָיו וְצִוָּנוּ עַל אֲכִילַת מַצָּה.

Blessed are You, Eternal our God, Ruler of the universe, Who made us holy with Your commandments and instructed us to eat the unleavened bread.

Directions: Both matzot are then broken into pieces the size of an olive (see page 107 for exact amount) and given to all participants, who eat them together while reclining to the left. Other matzot should be available to complete the required amounts; however, each participant should receive a piece from each of the top two matzot.

8. Maror מָרוֹר Eat the Bitter Herbs

We eat bitter herbs to remind us of the bitterness of slavery in Egypt. Charoset represents the clay and straw bricks with which the Israelites were forced to build the cities of Pithom and Ramses. We dip the bitter maror into the sweet charoset, as our ancestors tempered the bitterness of bondage with the sweet thoughts of redemption. The charoset also symbolizes the apple trees under which our foremothers gave birth, concealing their pain to avoid detection by the Egyptians

Directions: Leader(s) passes maror (romaine), charoset, broken pieces of the bottom matzah the size of an olive, and chazeret (pieces of horseradish). Each takes:
1) A piece of maror,
*2) Enough charoset for the blessing **and** the Hillel Sandwich (Korech) to follow,*
3) Two pieces from the bottom matzah for the Hillel Sandwich, and
4) A piece of chazeret (horseradish).

Since maror is a symbol of bondage, we do not recline while eating it. Each takes a portion of romaine, the size of an olive, and dips it into the charoset, shaking off most of the charoset so the bitter taste is not eliminated. Then eat the maror, after reciting the following blessing:

Baruch Ata Adonai, Eloheinu Melech Ha-olam, asher kid'shanu b'mitz'votav v'tzivanu al achilat maror.

בָּרוּךְ אַתָּה יְיָ אֱלֹהֵינוּ מֶלֶךְ הָעוֹלָם, אֲשֶׁר קִדְּשָׁנוּ בְּמִצְוֹתָיו וְצִוָּנוּ עַל אֲכִילַת מָרוֹר.

Blessed are You, Eternal our God, Ruler of the universe, Who made us holy by Your commandments and instructed us to eat the bitter herbs.

9. Korech כּוֹרֵךְ The Hillel Sandwich

> Hillel (1st century B.C.E.) was the greatest Sage of the Second Temple period. Noted for wisdom, humility, and teaching of leniency, he explained that mixing the bread of poverty/freedom with the bitter maror prevented any one taste from dominating another. The Korech Sandwich teaches us that those who are free must never forget the bitterness of enslavement; and those who are oppressed must keep the hope of freedom alive in their hearts.

Directions: One should concentrate on making the Korech (Hillel) sandwich of horseradish, charoset, and matzah, then reading and eating without delay.

While the Temple was still in existence, Hillel would make a sandwich of some bitter herbs, Passover Lamb and *matzah*, and eat them altogether, in order to fulfill the words of the Torah: "They shall eat it (the Passover Lamb) together with unleavened bread and bitter herbs." *(Ex. 12:8)*

זֵכֶר לְמִקְדָּשׁ כְּהִלֵּל: כֵּן עָשָׂה הִלֵּל בִּזְמַן שֶׁבֵּית הַמִּקְדָּשׁ הָיָה קַיָּם. הָיָה כּוֹרֵךְ פֶּסַח מַצָּה וּמָרוֹר וְאוֹכֵל בְּיַחַד. לְקַיֵּם מַה שֶּׁנֶּאֱמַר: עַל מַצּוֹת וּמְרֹרִים יֹאכְלֻהוּ.

Directions: Eat the Hillel Sandwich while reclining to the left.

10. Shul'chan Orech   שֻׁלְחָן עוֹרֵךְ   The Festival Meal

In many homes, it is customary to begin the meal with a hard-boiled egg, usually dipped in salt water, eaten while leaning to the left. This custom has numerous explanations. It is a symbol of mourning that commemorates the destruction of the Temple (Beit ha-Mikdash) where the Festival offering (chagigah) was brought. It also represents God's past desire to redeem us from slavery in Egypt and future desire to redeem us and rebuild the Temple. In addition, though most foods become softer when boiled, the egg becomes harder the more it is cooked. Like the egg, the more others try to oppress us, the more resistant we become to their efforts. The egg symbolizes that even a perfect egg must break for a new life to be born, just as the Israelites had to break away from their life of bondage in order to emerge as God's people.

When the Temple was in existence, roasted lamb was eaten at the Seder. Since the destruction of the Temple, lamb is not served, and *Ashkenazim* include nothing in the meal that has been roasted on an open flame.

Directions: *Remove the ritual symbols from the table.* THE MEAL IS SERVED

(Suggested menus and recipes can be found beginning on pages 112-123.)

11. Tzafun   צָפוּן   Eat the Afikoman

Directions: The meal cannot be ritually completed without eating the Afikoman, which symbolizes the Passover Sacrifice. The leader(s) redeems the Afikoman (the portion of the middle matzah that was hidden) from the child who finds it, and distributes an olive-size piece to all present, who eat it while reclining to the left.

It is customary to eat nothing else during the rest of the Seder, so that the taste of the *Afikoman*, which symbolizes the *Korban Pesach* (the Passover sacrifice of the Paschal lamb), remains undiluted in our mouths all night. Thus, we are not diverted from dwelling on the story of the Exodus from Egypt.

12. Barech   בָּרֵךְ   The Blessing After the Meal

Psalm 126, which introduces the *Birkat Hamazon*, describes the great joy of the exiles, twenty-five hundred years ago, after King Cyrus of Persia gave them permission to return from Babylonia to Judea and build a Holy Temple. Through the ages, this optimistic Psalm inspired Jews with hope for God's salvation, ultimate redemption and return to Zion.

Directions: Fill the third cup of wine and raise the cup in your right hand.

A Song of Ascents, Psalm 126   שִׁיר הַמַּעֲלוֹת   Shir HaMa-alot

Shir Hama-alot. B'shuv Adonai et shivat tzi-yon ha-yinu k'chol'mim. Az yimalei s'chok pinu ul'shonenu rina. Az yom'ru va-go-yim, hig'dil Adonai la-asot im eleh. Hig'dil Adonai la-asot imanu; ha-yinu s'mechim. Shuva Adonai et sh'vitenu ka-afikim banegev. Hazor'im b'dim'ah b'rina yik'tzoru. Haloch yelech u-vacho, nosei meshech hazara, bo yavo v'rina nosei alumotav.

שִׁיר הַמַּעֲלוֹת. בְּשׁוּב יְיָ אֶת שִׁיבַת צִיּוֹן הָיִינוּ כְּחֹלְמִים. אָז יִמָּלֵא שְׂחוֹק פִּינוּ וּלְשׁוֹנֵנוּ רִנָּה. אָז יֹאמְרוּ בַגּוֹיִם, הִגְדִּיל יְיָ לַעֲשׂוֹת עִם אֵלֶּה. הִגְדִּיל יְיָ לַעֲשׂוֹת עִמָּנוּ, הָיִינוּ שְׂמֵחִים: שׁוּבָה יְיָ אֶת שְׁבִיתֵנוּ כַּאֲפִיקִים בַּנֶּגֶב. הַזֹּרְעִים בְּדִמְעָה בְּרִנָּה יִקְצֹרוּ. הָלוֹךְ יֵלֵךְ וּבָכֹה נֹשֵׂא מֶשֶׁךְ הַזָּרַע, בֹּא יָבֹא בְרִנָּה נֹשֵׂא אֲלֻמֹּתָיו.

> When the Eternal brought our exiles back to Zion, we were like dreamers. Then our mouths were filled with laughter, our tongues with joyous song. Then it was said among the nations: "The Eternal has done great things for them." Yes, the Eternal did great things for us and we rejoiced. Return our exiles, O Eternal, like the flood streams in the desert. They who plant in tears shall harvest in joy. They who go forth weeping, bearing their seeds to the field, shall come home with songs of joy, bearing their sheaves of grain.

*Directions: From this point to the end of Birkat Hamazon, one should refrain from conversation. Grace after meals is a Torah commandment and is one of the most important parts of the Seder. When **three or more** have eaten together, the following introduction is added. When **ten or more** are present, the words in parentheses are added.*

Leader:

Chaverai n'varech.   חֲבֵרַי נְבָרֵךְ.

> Friends and family, let us give thanks for our food.

Participants, and then Leader:

Y'hi shem Adonai m'vorach me-ata v'ad olam.   יְהִי שֵׁם יְיָ מְבֹרָךְ מֵעַתָּה וְעַד עוֹלָם.

> May the name of the Eternal be blessed, now and forever.

Leader:

Bir'shut maranan v'rabanan v'rabotai, n'varech (Eloheinu) she-achal'nu mishelo.   בִּרְשׁוּת מָרָנָן וְרַבָּנָן וְרַבּוֹתַי, נְבָרֵךְ (אֱלֹהֵינוּ) שֶׁאָכַלְנוּ מִשֶּׁלּוֹ.

> With your consent, friends, let us praise God (our God), of Whose food we have eaten.

Participants, then Leader:

Baruch (Eloheinu) she-achal'nu mishelo, uv'tuvo cha-yinu.

בָּרוּךְ (אֱלֹהֵינוּ) שֶׁאָכַלְנוּ מִשֶּׁלּוֹ וּבְטוּבוֹ חָיִינוּ.

Blessed are You (our God) of Whose food we have eaten and through Whose goodness we live.

All:

Baruch Hu U-varuch Sh'mo.

בָּרוּךְ הוּא וּבָרוּךְ שְׁמוֹ.

Blessed are You and blessed is Your name.

First Blessing: For the Food

Baruch Ata Adonai, Eloheinu Melech Ha-olam, hazan et ha-olam kulo b'tuvo b'chen b'chesed uv'rachamim. Hu noten lechem l'chol basar, ki l'olam chas'do. Uv'tuvo hagadol tamid lo chasar lanu, v'al yech'sar lanu mazon l'olam va-ed, ba-avur sh'mo hagadol. Ki hu El zan um'farnes lakol u-metiv lakol u-mechin mazon l'chol b'ri-yotav asher bara. Baruch Ata Adonai, hazan et hakol.

בָּרוּךְ אַתָּה יְיָ אֱלֹהֵינוּ מֶלֶךְ הָעוֹלָם, הַזָּן אֶת הָעוֹלָם כֻּלּוֹ בְּטוּבוֹ בְּחֵן בְּחֶסֶד וּבְרַחֲמִים. הוּא נוֹתֵן לֶחֶם לְכָל בָּשָׂר כִּי לְעוֹלָם חַסְדּוֹ. וּבְטוּבוֹ הַגָּדוֹל תָּמִיד לֹא חָסַר לָנוּ, וְאַל יֶחְסַר לָנוּ מָזוֹן לְעוֹלָם וָעֶד. בַּעֲבוּר שְׁמוֹ הַגָּדוֹל, כִּי הוּא אֵל זָן וּמְפַרְנֵס לַכֹּל וּמֵטִיב לַכֹּל, וּמֵכִין מָזוֹן לְכֹל בְּרִיּוֹתָיו אֲשֶׁר בָּרָא. בָּרוּךְ אַתָּה יְיָ הַזָּן אֶת הַכֹּל.

Blessed are You, Eternal our God, Ruler of the universe, Who sustains the whole universe with grace, lovingkindness, and mercy. You provide food for every creature, for Your kindness endures forever. In Your great goodness, we have never been in want and may we never lack sustenance forever and ever, for the sake of Your great name. All life is Your creation and You are good to all, providing every creature with food and sustenance. Blessed are You, Eternal, Who sustains all life.

*Directions: The complete version of **Birkat Hamazon** follows. For the shorter version, please turn to page 69.*

Second Blessing: For the Land

We thank You, Eternal our God, for the good, pleasant, and spacious land which You gave to our ancestors as an inheritance; and because You, O Eternal our God, liberated us from the land of Egypt and redeemed us from the house of bondage; and for Your covenant sealed in our flesh; and for Your Torah which You taught us; and for Your laws which You made known to us; and for the life, favor and kindness which You granted us, and for the food we eat, with which You constantly nourish and sustain us, every day, at all times and at every hour.

For all this, Eternal our God, we thank You and we bless You. May Your name be blessed by every living being continually and forever. As it is written: "When you have eaten and are satisfied, you shall bless the Eternal your God for the good land which God has given you." *(Deut. 8:10)* Blessed are You, Eternal, for the land and for its food.

נוֹדֶה לְךָ יְיָ אֱלֹהֵינוּ עַל שֶׁהִנְחַלְתָּ לַאֲבוֹתֵינוּ, אֶרֶץ חֶמְדָּה טוֹבָה וּרְחָבָה, וְעַל שֶׁהוֹצֵאתָנוּ יְיָ אֱלֹהֵינוּ מֵאֶרֶץ מִצְרַיִם, וּפְדִיתָנוּ, מִבֵּית עֲבָדִים, וְעַל בְּרִיתְךָ שֶׁחָתַמְתָּ בִּבְשָׂרֵנוּ, וְעַל תּוֹרָתְךָ שֶׁלִּמַּדְתָּנוּ, וְעַל חֻקֶּיךָ שֶׁהוֹדַעְתָּנוּ וְעַל חַיִּים חֵן וָחֶסֶד שֶׁחוֹנַנְתָּנוּ, וְעַל אֲכִילַת מָזוֹן שָׁאַתָּה זָן וּמְפַרְנֵס אוֹתָנוּ תָּמִיד, בְּכָל יוֹם וּבְכָל עֵת וּבְכָל שָׁעָה.

וְעַל הַכֹּל יְיָ אֱלֹהֵינוּ אֲנַחְנוּ מוֹדִים לָךְ, וּמְבָרְכִים אוֹתָךְ, יִתְבָּרַךְ שִׁמְךָ בְּפִי כָּל חַי תָּמִיד לְעוֹלָם וָעֶד. כַּכָּתוּב, וְאָכַלְתָּ, וְשָׂבָעְתָּ, וּבֵרַכְתָּ אֶת יְיָ אֱלֹהֶיךָ, עַל הָאָרֶץ הַטֹּבָה אֲשֶׁר נָתַן לָךְ. בָּרוּךְ אַתָּה יְיָ עַל הָאָרֶץ וְעַל הַמָּזוֹן.

Third Blessing: For Jerusalem

Have mercy, Eternal our God, on Your people Israel, on Your city Jerusalem and Zion—the dwelling place of Your glory, on the royal house of David, Your anointed, and on the great and holy Temple called by Your name. Our God, our Parent, tend and nourish us, sustain and support us, and O Eternal God, speedily grant us relief from all our troubles. Eternal our God, let us not be in need of gifts from others or their favors, but only of Your full, open, generous and holy hand, so that we may never be shamed or humiliated.

רַחֵם יְיָ אֱלֹהֵינוּ, עַל יִשְׂרָאֵל עַמֶּךָ, וְעַל יְרוּשָׁלַיִם עִירֶךָ, וְעַל צִיּוֹן מִשְׁכַּן כְּבוֹדֶךָ, וְעַל מַלְכוּת בֵּית דָּוִד מְשִׁיחֶךָ, וְעַל הַבַּיִת הַגָּדוֹל וְהַקָּדוֹשׁ שֶׁנִּקְרָא שִׁמְךָ עָלָיו. אֱלֹהֵינוּ, אָבִינוּ רְעֵנוּ, זוּנֵנוּ, פַּרְנְסֵנוּ, וְכַלְכְּלֵנוּ וְהַרְוִיחֵנוּ, וְהַרְוַח לָנוּ יְיָ אֱלֹהֵינוּ מְהֵרָה מִכָּל צָרוֹתֵינוּ. וְנָא אַל תַּצְרִיכֵנוּ יְיָ אֱלֹהֵינוּ, לֹא לִידֵי מַתְּנַת בָּשָׂר וָדָם, וְלֹא לִידֵי הַלְוָאָתָם, כִּי אִם לְיָדְךָ הַמְּלֵאָה, הַפְּתוּחָה, הַקְּדוֹשָׁה וְהָרְחָבָה, שֶׁלֹּא נֵבוֹשׁ וְלֹא נִכָּלֵם לְעוֹלָם וָעֶד.

On the Sabbath, add this paragraph:

Favor us, Eternal our God, and strengthen us with Your commandments, especially in the observance of the seventh day, this great and holy Sabbath. It is a great and holy day lovingly given by You for rest and serenity. Eternal our God, spare us from trouble, grief or anguish on our day of rest. Grant that we may soon behold the comforting of Zion, Your city, and the rebuilding of Jerusalem, Your holy city, for You are the God of salvation and of consolation.

רְצֵה וְהַחֲלִיצֵנוּ יְיָ אֱלֹהֵינוּ בְּמִצְוֹתֶיךָ, וּבְמִצְוַת יוֹם הַשְּׁבִיעִי הַשַּׁבָּת הַגָּדוֹל וְהַקָּדוֹשׁ הַזֶּה, כִּי יוֹם זֶה גָּדוֹל וְקָדוֹשׁ הוּא לְפָנֶיךָ, לִשְׁבָּת בּוֹ וְלָנוּחַ בּוֹ בְּאַהֲבָה כְּמִצְוַת רְצוֹנֶךָ. וּבִרְצוֹנְךָ הָנִיחַ לָנוּ יְיָ אֱלֹהֵינוּ, שֶׁלֹּא תְהֵא צָרָה וְיָגוֹן וַאֲנָחָה בְּיוֹם מְנוּחָתֵנוּ. וְהַרְאֵנוּ יְיָ אֱלֹהֵינוּ בְּנֶחָמַת צִיּוֹן עִירֶךָ, וּבְבִנְיַן יְרוּשָׁלַיִם עִיר קָדְשֶׁךָ, כִּי אַתָּה הוּא בַּעַל הַיְשׁוּעוֹת וּבַעַל הַנֶּחָמוֹת.

Our God and God of our ancestors, may You favor and remember us and our ancestors. Remember the Messiah, son of David, Your servant, and Jerusalem, Your holy City, and all Your people Israel. Grant us life, well being, kindliness, compassion and peace on this Festival of Matzot. Bless us, Eternal our God, with all that is good. Remember, with compassion, Your promise of mercy and redemption. Favor us and save us, for we turn our eyes to You alone, gracious and merciful God and Sovereign.

אֱלֹהֵינוּ וֵאלֹהֵי אֲבוֹתֵינוּ, יַעֲלֶה וְיָבֹא וְיַגִּיעַ, וְיֵרָאֶה, וְיֵרָצֶה, וְיִשָּׁמַע, וְיִפָּקֵד וְיִזָּכֵר זִכְרוֹנֵנוּ וּפִקְדוֹנֵנוּ, וְזִכְרוֹן אֲבוֹתֵינוּ, וְזִכְרוֹן מָשִׁיחַ בֶּן דָּוִד עַבְדֶּךָ, וְזִכְרוֹן יְרוּשָׁלַיִם עִיר קָדְשֶׁךָ, וְזִכְרוֹן כָּל עַמְּךָ בֵּית יִשְׂרָאֵל לְפָנֶיךָ, לִפְלֵיטָה לְטוֹבָה לְחֵן וּלְחֶסֶד וּלְרַחֲמִים, לְחַיִּים וּלְשָׁלוֹם בְּיוֹם חַג הַמַּצּוֹת הַזֶּה. זָכְרֵנוּ יְיָ אֱלֹהֵינוּ בּוֹ לְטוֹבָה, וּפָקְדֵנוּ בוֹ לִבְרָכָה, וְהוֹשִׁיעֵנוּ בוֹ לְחַיִּים. וּבִדְבַר יְשׁוּעָה וְרַחֲמִים, חוּס וְחָנֵּנוּ וְרַחֵם עָלֵינוּ וְהוֹשִׁיעֵנוּ, כִּי אֵלֶיךָ עֵינֵינוּ, כִּי אֵל מֶלֶךְ חַנּוּן וְרַחוּם אָתָּה.

Rebuild Jerusalem, Your holy City, speedily in our lifetime. Blessed are You, Eternal, Who in Your mercy will rebuild Jerusalem. Amen.

וּבְנֵה יְרוּשָׁלַיִם עִיר הַקֹּדֶשׁ בִּמְהֵרָה בְיָמֵינוּ. בָּרוּךְ אַתָּה יְיָ בּוֹנֵה בְרַחֲמָיו יְרוּשָׁלָיִם. אָמֵן.

Fourth Blessing: God's Goodness

Blessed are You, Eternal our God, Ruler of the universe, our Parent, our Ruler, our Sovereign, our Creator and Redeemer, our Maker, our Holy One and the Holy One of

בָּרוּךְ אַתָּה יְיָ אֱלֹהֵינוּ מֶלֶךְ הָעוֹלָם, הָאֵל אָבִינוּ, מַלְכֵּנוּ, אַדִּירֵנוּ, בּוֹרְאֵנוּ, גּוֹאֲלֵנוּ, יוֹצְרֵנוּ, קְדוֹשֵׁנוּ, קְדוֹשׁ יַעֲקֹב,

Jacob, Rachel and Leah. You are our Shepherd and Shepherd of Israel, the Sovereign Who is good to all, Whose goodness is constant throughout all time. As You have blessed us and are blessing us, may You continue to bless us forever with Your grace, kindness, mercy, deliverance, security, success, blessing, salvation, consolation, sustenance, support, life and peace and all that is good. May we never lack any goodness.

רָחֵל וְלֵאָה, רוֹעֵנוּ רוֹעֵה יִשְׂרָאֵל, הַמֶּלֶךְ הַטּוֹב, וְהַמֵּטִיב לַכֹּל, שֶׁבְּכָל יוֹם וָיוֹם הוּא הֵטִיב, הוּא מֵטִיב, הוּא יֵיטִיב לָנוּ. הוּא גְמָלָנוּ, הוּא גוֹמְלֵנוּ, הוּא יִגְמְלֵנוּ לָעַד, לְחֵן וּלְחֶסֶד וּלְרַחֲמִים וּלְרֶוַח הַצָּלָה וְהַצְלָחָה, בְּרָכָה וִישׁוּעָה, נֶחָמָה פַּרְנָסָה וְכַלְכָּלָה, וְרַחֲמִים וְחַיִּים וְשָׁלוֹם וְכָל טוֹב, וּמִכָּל טוּב לְעוֹלָם אַל יְחַסְּרֵנוּ.

May the All Merciful rule over us forever.

הָרַחֲמָן, הוּא יִמְלוֹךְ עָלֵינוּ לְעוֹלָם וָעֶד.

May the All Merciful be blessed in heaven and on earth.

הָרַחֲמָן, הוּא יִתְבָּרַךְ בַּשָּׁמַיִם וּבָאָרֶץ.

May the All Merciful be praised for all generations and glorified and honored among us for all eternity.

הָרַחֲמָן, הוּא יִשְׁתַּבַּח לְדוֹר דּוֹרִים, וְיִתְפָּאַר בָּנוּ לָעַד וּלְנֵצַח נְצָחִים, וְיִתְהַדַּר בָּנוּ לָעַד וּלְעוֹלְמֵי עוֹלָמִים.

May the All Merciful grant us an honorable livelihood.

הָרַחֲמָן, הוּא יְפַרְנְסֵנוּ בְּכָבוֹד.

May the All Merciful end our oppression and lead us proudly to our homeland.

הָרַחֲמָן, הוּא יִשְׁבּוֹר עֻלֵּנוּ מֵעַל צַוָּארֵנוּ, וְהוּא יוֹלִיכֵנוּ קוֹמְמִיּוּת לְאַרְצֵנוּ.

May the All Merciful grant abundant blessings on this household and upon all who have eaten at this table.

הָרַחֲמָן, הוּא יִשְׁלַח לָנוּ בְּרָכָה מְרֻבָּה בַּבַּיִת הַזֶּה, וְעַל שֻׁלְחָן זֶה שֶׁאָכַלְנוּ עָלָיו.

May the All Merciful send us Elijah, the Prophet, of blessed memory, and may he announce to us good tidings of salvation and comfort.

הָרַחֲמָן, הוּא יִשְׁלַח לָנוּ אֶת אֵלִיָּהוּ הַנָּבִיא זָכוּר לַטּוֹב, וִיבַשֶּׂר לָנוּ בְּשׂוֹרוֹת טוֹבוֹת יְשׁוּעוֹת וְנֶחָמוֹת.

When eating at your parents' table:
May the All Merciful bless my honored father and teacher and my esteemed mother and teacher, the heads of this household, and all that is theirs.

הָרַחֲמָן, הוּא יְבָרֵךְ אֶת אָבִי מוֹרִי בַּעַל הַבַּיִת הַזֶּה, וְאֶת אִמִּי מוֹרָתִי בַּעֲלַת הַבַּיִת הַזֶּה, אוֹתָם וְאֶת בֵּיתָם וְאֶת זַרְעָם וְאֶת כָּל אֲשֶׁר לָהֶם.

A Wife or Husband says:

May the All Merciful bless me, (my wife/my husband, my children), and all that is mine.

הָרַחֲמָן, הוּא יְבָרֵךְ אוֹתִי (וְאֶת אִשְׁתִּי) (וְאֶת אִישִׁי) (וְאֶת זַרְעִי) וְאֶת כָּל אֲשֶׁר לִי.

A Guest says:

May the All Merciful bless our hosts, their household, their children, their endeavors and all that is theirs.

הָרַחֲמָן, הוּא יְבָרֵךְ אֶת בַּעַל הַבַּיִת הַזֶּה, וְאֶת אִשְׁתּוֹ בַּעֲלַת הַבַּיִת הַזֶּה. אוֹתָם וְאֶת בֵּיתָם וְאֶת זַרְעָם וְאֶת כָּל אֲשֶׁר לָהֶם.

All Together:

May the All Merciful bless us and all that is ours, as God blessed our ancestors, Abraham and Sarah, Isaac and Rebecca, and Jacob, Rachel and Leah, in everything. May God bless us all together, fully, and let us say: Amen.

הָרַחֲמָן, הוּא יְבָרֵךְ אוֹתָנוּ וְאֶת כָּל אֲשֶׁר לָנוּ, כְּמוֹ שֶׁנִּתְבָּרְכוּ אֲבוֹתֵינוּ, אַבְרָהָם וְשָׂרָה, יִצְחָק וְרִבְקָה, וְיַעֲקֹב רָחֵל וְלֵאָה בַּכֹּל מִכֹּל כֹּל, כֵּן יְבָרֵךְ אוֹתָנוּ כֻּלָּנוּ יַחַד. בִּבְרָכָה שְׁלֵמָה, וְנֹאמַר, אָמֵן.

May we secure enduring peace through the merit of our ancestors and ourselves. May we receive blessings from the Eternal, and kindness from the God of our salvation. May we find grace and favor in the eyes of God and of all people.

בַּמָּרוֹם יְלַמְּדוּ עֲלֵיהֶם וְעָלֵינוּ זְכוּת, שֶׁתְּהֵא לְמִשְׁמֶרֶת שָׁלוֹם. וְנִשָּׂא בְרָכָה מֵאֵת יְיָ, וּצְדָקָה מֵאֱלֹהֵי יִשְׁעֵנוּ, וְנִמְצָא חֵן וְשֵׂכֶל טוֹב בְּעֵינֵי אֱלֹהִים וְאָדָם.

On the Sabbath, add the following sentence:

May the All Merciful grant us a day of uninterrupted Sabbath tranquility in eternal life.

הָרַחֲמָן, הוּא יַנְחִילֵנוּ יוֹם שֶׁכֻּלּוֹ שַׁבָּת וּמְנוּחָה לְחַיֵּי הָעוֹלָמִים.

Continue:

May the All Merciful grant us a day when complete goodness prevails.

וּלְחַיֵּי הָעוֹלָם הַבָּא.

May the All Merciful find us worthy of seeing the days of the Messiah and of eternal life in the world to come.

הָרַחֲמָן, הוּא יַנְחִילֵנוּ יוֹם שֶׁכֻּלּוֹ טוֹב. הָרַחֲמָן, הוּא יְזַכֵּנוּ לִימוֹת הַמָּשִׁיחַ

מִגְדוֹל יְשׁוּעוֹת מַלְכּוֹ וְעֹשֶׂה חֶסֶד לִמְשִׁיחוֹ לְדָוִד וּלְזַרְעוֹ עַד עוֹלָם.

You are a tower of salvation and kindness to David, Your anointed king, and his descendents forever.

עֹשֶׂה שָׁלוֹם בִּמְרוֹמָיו, הוּא יַעֲשֶׂה שָׁלוֹם עָלֵינוּ וְעַל כָּל יִשְׂרָאֵל, וְאִמְרוּ אָמֵן.

May the Creator, Who makes peace in the heavens, grant peace to us and to all Israel, and let us say, Amen.

יְראוּ אֶת יְיָ קְדֹשָׁיו, כִּי אֵין מַחְסוֹר לִירֵאָיו. כְּפִירִים רָשׁוּ וְרָעֵבוּ, וְדוֹרְשֵׁי יְיָ לֹא יַחְסְרוּ כָל טוֹב. הוֹדוּ לַיְיָ כִּי טוֹב, כִּי לְעוֹלָם חַסְדּוֹ. פּוֹתֵחַ אֶת יָדֶךָ, וּמַשְׂבִּיעַ לְכָל חַי רָצוֹן. בָּרוּךְ הַגֶּבֶר אֲשֶׁר יִבְטַח בַּיְיָ, וְהָיָה יְיָ מִבְטַחוֹ. נַעַר הָיִיתִי גַּם זָקַנְתִּי, וְלֹא רָאִיתִי צַדִּיק נֶעֱזָב, וְזַרְעוֹ מְבַקֶּשׁ לָחֶם. יְיָ עֹז לְעַמּוֹ יִתֵּן, יְיָ יְבָרֵךְ אֶת עַמּוֹ בַשָּׁלוֹם.

Revere the Eternal, God's holy ones, for those who revere God suffer no want. Even young lions may suffer want and hunger, but those who seek the Eternal shall not lack for any good. Give thanks to the Eternal, for God is good. God's kindness endures forever. You open Your hand and satisfy the desire of every living thing. Blessed is the person who trusts in the Eternal and whose security is the Eternal. Once I was young, now I am old; yet I have never seen the righteous abandoned, nor their children begging for bread. The Eternal will give strength to us and bless us with peace.

*The **short version** of **Birkat Hamazon** follows. Start with Shir Hama-alot on page 63, following the directions through page 64. Then continue here.*

Second Blessing for the Land

נוֹדֶה לְךָ יְיָ אֱלֹהֵינוּ עַל שֶׁהִנְחַלְתָּ לַאֲבוֹתֵינוּ, אֶרֶץ חֶמְדָּה טוֹבָה וּרְחָבָה, בְּרִית וְתוֹרָה, חַיִּים וּמָזוֹן. יִתְבָּרַךְ שִׁמְךָ בְּפִי כָּל חַי תָּמִיד לְעוֹלָם וָעֶד. כַּכָּתוּב, וְאָכַלְתָּ וְשָׂבָעְתָּ, וּבֵרַכְתָּ אֶת יְיָ אֱלֹהֶיךָ עַל הָאָרֶץ הַטֹּבָה אֲשֶׁר נָתַן לָךְ. בָּרוּךְ אַתָּה יְיָ עַל הָאָרֶץ וְעַל הַמָּזוֹן.

Nodeh l'cha Adonai Eloheinu al she-hin'chal'ta la-avoteinu eretz chem'da tovah ur'chava, b'rit v'torah, chayim u-mazon. Yit'barach shim'cha b'fi kol chai tamid l'olam va-ed. Kakatuv v'a-chal'ta v'sava'ta u-verach'ta et Adonai Elohecha al ha-aretz hatovah asher natan lach. Baruch Ata Adonaoi, al ha-aretz v'al hamazon.

We thank You, Eternal our God, for the good, desirable, and spacious land which You gave to our ancestors as an inheritance; and because You, O Eternal our God, liberated us from the land of Egypt and redeemed us from the house of bondage; and for Your covenant sealed in our flesh; and for Your Torah which You taught us; and Your laws which You made known to us; and for the gift of life which You have bestowed upon us with grace and kindness, and for the food we eat with which You constantly nourish and sustain us, every day, at all times and at every hour. May You forever be blessed by all who live, as it is written in the Torah: "When you have eaten and are satisfied, you shall bless your Eternal God for the good land which God has given you." *(Deut. 8:10)* Blessed are You, Eternal, for the land and for the food.

Third Blessing: For Jerusalem

Rachem Adonai Eloheinu al Yis'ra-el amecha. V'al mal'chut beit David m'shi-checha. Uv'neh Y'rusha-layim ir hakodesh bim'herah v'yameinu. Baruch Ata Adonai, boneh b'rachamav Y'rusha-layim. Amen.

רַחֵם יְיָ אֱלֹהֵינוּ, עַל יִשְׂרָאֵל עַמֶּךָ, וְעַל מַלְכוּת בֵּית דָּוִד מְשִׁיחֶךָ, וּבְנֵה יְרוּשָׁלַיִם עִיר הַקֹּדֶשׁ בִּמְהֵרָה בְיָמֵינוּ. בָּרוּךְ אַתָּה יְיָ בּוֹנֵה בְרַחֲמָיו יְרוּשָׁלָיִם. אָמֵן.

Have mercy, Eternal our God, upon Your people Israel and upon the royal house of David, Your anointed. Rebuild Jerusalem, Your holy City, speedily in our lifetime. Blessed are You, Eternal, Who in Your mercy rebuilds Jerusalem. Amen.

Fourth Blessing: God's Goodness

Baruch Ata Adonai, Eloheinu Melech Ha-olam, hamelech hatov v'hametiv lakol. Hu hetiv, hu metiv, hu yeitiv lanu, hu g'ma-lanu hu gom'lenu hu yig'm'lenu la-ad chen va-chesed v'rachamim, vi-zakenu limot hamashi-ach.

בָּרוּךְ אַתָּה יְיָ אֱלֹהֵינוּ מֶלֶךְ הָעוֹלָם, הַמֶּלֶךְ הַטּוֹב וְהַמֵּטִיב לַכֹּל. הוּא הֵטִיב, הוּא מֵטִיב, הוּא יֵיטִיב לָנוּ. הוּא גְמָלָנוּ, הוּא גוֹמְלֵנוּ, הוּא יִגְמְלֵנוּ לָעַד חֵן וָחֶסֶד וְרַחֲמִים וִיזַכֵּנוּ לִימוֹת הַמָּשִׁיחַ.

Blessed are You, Eternal our God, Ruler of the universe, Who is good to all, Whose goodness is constant throughout all time. Favor us with loving kindness and mercy, now and in the future as You did in the past. May we be worthy of witnessing the days of the Messiah.

Harachaman Hu Y'varech et kol ham'subin kan.

הָרַחֲמָן, הוּא יְבָרֵךְ אֶת כָּל הַמְסֻבִּין כָּאן.

May the All Merciful bless all who are gathered here.

On the Sabbath, add the following sentences:

Harachaman hu yan'chilenu yom shekulo Shabbat um'nucha l'chayei ha-olamim.

הָרַחֲמָן, הוּא יַנְחִילֵנוּ יוֹם שֶׁכֻּלוֹ שַׁבָּת וּמְנוּחָה לְחַיֵּי הָעוֹלָמִים.

> May the All Merciful grant us a day of uninterrupted Sabbath tranquility in eternal life.

Continue:

Harachaman hu yan'chilenu yom she-kulo tov.

הָרַחֲמָן, הוּא יַנְחִילֵנוּ יוֹם שֶׁכֻּלוֹ טוֹב.

> May the All Merciful grant us a day when complete goodness prevails.

V'nisa v'racha me-et Adonai utz'dakah me-Elohei yish'enu v'nimtza chen v'sechel tov b'einei Elohim v'adam. Oseh shalom bim'romav hu ya-aseh shalom aleinu v'al kol Yis'ra-el V'imru, Amen.

וְנִשָּׂא בְרָכָה מֵאֵת יְיָ וּצְדָקָה מֵאֱלֹהֵי יִשְׁעֵנוּ וְנִמְצָא חֵן וְשֵׂכֶל טוֹב בְּעֵינֵי אֱלֹהִים וְאָדָם. עֹשֶׂה שָׁלוֹם בִּמְרוֹמָיו, הוּא יַעֲשֶׂה שָׁלוֹם, עָלֵינוּ וְעַל כָּל יִשְׂרָאֵל, וְאִמְרוּ אָמֵן.

> May we receive blessings from the Eternal, and righteousness from the God of our salvation. May we find grace and understanding in the eyes of God and of all people. May the Creator, Who makes peace in the heavens, grant peace to us and to all Israel, and let us say, Amen.

United Synagogue of America, 1979 (adapted)

Directions: After saying the blessing, drink from the third cup of wine while reclining to the left.

Baruch Ata Adonai, Eloheinu Melech Ha-olam, borei p'ri hagafen.

בָּרוּךְ אַתָּה יְיָ אֱלֹהֵינוּ מֶלֶךְ הָעוֹלָם, בּוֹרֵא פְּרִי הַגָּפֶן.

> Blessed are You, Eternal our God, Ruler of the universe, Who creates the fruit of the vine.

Directions: The fourth cup of wine is filled. If you have tambourines or noise makers, pass them out to guests now.

The Cup of Elijah and the Cup of Miriam

No other character in Jewish History is so surrounded by mystery, legend, and hope as Elijah. According to tradition, at the end of his earthly life, Elijah ascended to heaven in a fiery chariot. In Jewish legends, Elijah is the protector of the Jewish people, champion of the oppressed, and performer of miracles. Most importantly, our Sages say that in the month of *Nisan*, Elijah will announce the coming of the Messiah, when total human freedom will reign supreme. But Elijah will come only when we have adequately prepared the way for him, when "Nation shall not lift up sword against nation, neither shall they learn war anymore."

Our Sages say: "By virtue of the righteous women of that generation, the Israelites were redeemed from Egypt." We honor Miriam, the sister of Moses, who prophesied his birth, watched over him, and suggested her mother, Yocheved, as his wet nurse to the Pharaoh's daughter. As the Israelites entered the divided waters of the Reed Sea, Miriam, the prophet, led the women in song and dance.

Directions: Sing **Miriam's Song** *(Based on Exodus 15:20-21)*

Chorus:
And the women dancing with their timbrels
Followed Miriam as she sang her song.
Sing a song to the One whom we've exalted
Miriam and the women danced and danced the whole night long.

And Miriam was a weaver of unique variety.
The tapestry she wove was one, which sang our history.
With every thread and every strand she crafted her delight.
A woman touched with spirit, she dances toward the light. **Chorus:**

As Miriam stood upon the shores and gazed across the sea,
The wonder of this miracle she soon came to believe.
Whoever thought the sea would part with an outstretched hand,
And we would pass to freedom, and march to the Promised Land. **Chorus:**

And Miriam the Prophet took her timbrel in her hand,
And all the women followed her just as she had planned.
And Miriam raised her voice with song.
She sang with praise and might,
We've just lived through a miracle; we're going to dance tonight. **Chorus:**

Lyrics by Debbie Friedman

While Elijah's Cup represents our future redemption when the Messianic age will bring universal peace, Miriam's Cup is a symbol of our past redemption when our people were brought out of Egypt and delivered from slavery. Just as our people were sustained in the desert and transformed until they became a new people, so may we be delivered, sustained and transformed on our journey to a stronger sense of ourselves as individuals and as one people.

As each person pours a little of his/her wine into Elijah's cup and a little of his/her water into Miriam's cup, we begin to act together to bring about the Messianic era. The Sages state: "Israel will not be redeemed **except** through its own efforts."

Leader:

Let us <u>open the door</u> to express our belief in the coming of the Messiah and <u>rise</u> in the hope that Elijah will enter. With the greeting reserved for the most distinguished guests, let us say:

All together:
Baruch haba.

ברוּךְ הַבָּא

Blessed be he who comes.

Leader:

Let us sing the song of Elijah and pray that we may soon see his hope of a world of freedom and peace for all humankind.

E-li-yahu ha-navi, E-li-yahu ha-Tish'bi, E-li-yahu, E-li-yahu, E-li-yahu ha-Gil'adi; bim'he-ra v'ya-meinu, yavo e-leinu im mashi-ach ben David, im mashi-ach ben David.

אֵלִיָּהוּ הַנָּבִיא, אֵלִיָּהוּ הַתִּשְׁבִּי, אֵלִיָּהוּ,
אֵלִיָּהוּ, אֵלִיָּהוּ הַגִּלְעָדִי, בִּמְהֵרָה בְיָמֵינוּ
יָבֹא אֵלֵינוּ עִם מָשִׁיחַ בֶּן דָּוִד, עִם
מָשִׁיחַ בֶּן דָּוִד.

Elijah, the Prophet; Elijah, the Tishbite; Elijah, the Gileadite; may he soon come and bring the Messiah.

Directions: Be seated

What can I do to hasten that day?

I can learn as I look at differences,
People aren't so different at all.
I can learn the need for learning
To solve problems—great and small;
    And that brings us nearer to redemption.

I must learn if I would have freedom,
I must want for others no less.
I must learn the need for learning
How to give to the world my best;
    And that means working for redemption.

And if I can use my learning
To understand friend and foe,
And bring about harmony and peoplehood,
Though the process may be slow,
    I'll have earned my redemption.

Imagine—no wars or famine!
No prejudice, injustice, or hate—
But a world of loving and learning!
It really isn't too late—
    For the realization of redemption.

E. Ramonia Longs

"Pour out your wrath...": are Torah verses that ask God to destroy the enemies of the Jewish people. It is here that we acknowledge our anger and pain for the many great wrongs done to the Jewish people by the recurring cycle of anti-Semitism. Our expression of anger, however, is part of a process to take us beyond the pain and begin to heal the world.

Pour out Your wrath upon the nations that do not recognize You, and upon the governments that do not call upon Your Name; for they have devoured Jacob, Rachel and Leah, and destroyed their dwelling place. *(Ps. 79:6,7)* Pour out Your rage upon them and let Your burning fury overtake them. *(Ps. 69:25)* Pursue them with anger and destroy them from under the heavens of the Eternal. *(Lam. 3:66)*

שְׁפֹךְ חֲמָתְךָ אֶל הַגּוֹיִם אֲשֶׁר לֹא
יְדָעוּךָ וְעַל מַמְלָכוֹת אֲשֶׁר בְּשִׁמְךָ
לֹא קָרָאוּ. כִּי אָכַל אֶת יַעֲקֹב רָחֵל
וְלֵאָה וְאֶת נָוֵהוּ הֵשַׁמּוּ. שְׁפָךְ עֲלֵיהֶם
זַעְמֶךָ, וַחֲרוֹן אַפְּךָ יַשִּׂיגֵם. תִּרְדֹּף
בְּאַף וְתַשְׁמִידֵם מִתַּחַת שְׁמֵי יְיָ.

On this Seder night, we remember with reverence and love the six millions of our people from Europe who perished at the hands of a tyrant more wicked than the Pharaoh. "Come," he said to his followers, "let us cut them off from being a people, and the name of Israel shall be forgotten." And they slew the blameless and pure—men, women and children—with vapors of poison and burned them with fire.

Now, on the first day of Passover, the remnants of our people who were left in the Ghetto of Warsaw rose up against the wicked ones for the sanctification of God's name, and slew many of them before they died, even as in the days of Judah the Maccabee. They were beautiful in their lives, and united in their deaths. They brought redemption to the name of Israel throughout the world.

> There are stars whose radiance is visible
>   on earth though they have long been extinct.
> There are people whose brilliance continues to light
>   the world though they are no longer among the
>   living.
> These lights are particularly bright when the night is dark.
> They light the way for [hu]mankind.
>
> *Hannah Senesh*

> We who lived in concentration camps can remember the people who walked through the huts comforting others, giving away their last piece of bread. They may have been few in number, but they offer sufficient proof that everything can be taken from [an individual] but one thing: the last of the human freedoms—to choose one's attitude in any given set of circumstances, to choose one's own way.
>
> *Viktor E. Frankl**

Directions: The door is closed.

As we mourn our people's tragic fate, we also recall with admiration and gratitude the compassionate men and women of other faiths and nationalities who, at the peril of their lives, protected and saved thousands of Jews.[36]

Ani ma-amin be-emuna sh'lema, b'vi-at hamashi-ach, v'af al pi sheyit'mah'me-ah, im kol zeh achakeh lo, b'chol yom, she-yavo.

אֲנִי מַאֲמִין בֶּאֱמוּנָה שְׁלֵמָה בְּבִיאַת הַמָּשִׁיחַ, וְאַף עַל פִּי שֶׁיִּתְמַהְמֵהַּ, עִם כָּל זֶה אֲחַכֶּה לוֹ, בְּכָל יוֹם, שֶׁיָּבֹא.

> I believe with perfect faith in the coming of the Messiah; and though you may tarry, I await your coming daily.

*Additional literature on the Holocaust can be found on page 106.

13. Hallel   הַלֵּל   Psalms of Praise, Psalms 115-118

We praise God for nature, for truth, for safety and for freedom.

The first part of the Seder deals mainly with our redemption from Egypt, closing with the first two psalms of the *Hallel* (Psalms 113, 114). The meal serves as a transition between the past and the future.

    The second part of the Seder is devoted to our future national and universal redemption. We conclude with *Nishmat*, in which we pray that all nations praise the God of Israel.[37]

PSALM 115:1-11 *Responsive Reading*

Not to us, O Eternal, not to us	לֹא לָנוּ יְיָ לֹא לָנוּ,
But to Your name give glory,	כִּי לְשִׁמְךָ תֵּן כָּבוֹד,
For Your mercy and truth.	עַל חַסְדְּךָ עַל אֲמִתֶּךָ.
Why should the nations taunt us, saying,	לָמָּה יֹאמְרוּ הַגּוֹיִם,
"Where now is their God?"	אַיֵּה נָא אֱלֹהֵיהֶם.
Our God is in heaven,	וֵאלֹהֵינוּ בַשָּׁמָיִם כֹּל
Doing what the Eternal desires.	אֲשֶׁר חָפֵץ עָשָׂה.
Their idols are mere silver and gold,	עֲצַבֵּיהֶם כֶּסֶף וְזָהָב,
The work of human hands.	מַעֲשֵׂה יְדֵי אָדָם.
They have mouths, but speak not.	פֶּה לָהֶם וְלֹא יְדַבֵּרוּ,
They have eyes, but see not.	עֵינַיִם לָהֶם וְלֹא יִרְאוּ.
They have ears, but hear not.	אָזְנַיִם לָהֶם וְלֹא יִשְׁמָעוּ,
They have noses, but smell not.	אַף לָהֶם וְלֹא יְרִיחוּן.
They have hands, but feel not.	יְדֵיהֶם וְלֹא יְמִישׁוּן,
They have feet, but walk not.	רַגְלֵיהֶם וְלֹא יְהַלֵּכוּ,
They utter no sound in their throats.	לֹא יֶהְגּוּ בִּגְרוֹנָם.
Those who make them are like them,	כְּמוֹהֶם יִהְיוּ עֹשֵׂיהֶם,
And everyone who trusts in them.	כֹּל אֲשֶׁר בֹּטֵחַ בָּהֶם.
Let Israel trust in the Eternal.	יִשְׂרָאֵל בְּטַח בַּיְיָ, עֶזְרָם
God is your help and shield.	וּמָגִנָּם הוּא. בֵּית אַהֲרֹן בִּטְחוּ
Let the house of Aaron trust in the Eternal.	בַיְיָ, עֶזְרָם וּמָגִנָּם הוּא.
God is your help and shield.	
You who revere the Eternal trust in the Eternal.	יִרְאֵי יְיָ בִּטְחוּ בַיְיָ,
God is your help and shield.	עֶזְרָם וּמָגִנָּם הוּא.

PSALM 115: 12-18 *Responsive Reading*

The Eternal Who remembers us will bless us;
God will bless the house of Israel and the House of Aaron.
> Blessed are those who revere the Eternal,
> The lowly and the great alike.

יְיָ זְכָרָנוּ יְבָרֵךְ,
יְבָרֵךְ אֶת בֵּית יִשְׂרָאֵל,
יְבָרֵךְ אֶת בֵּית אַהֲרֹן.
יְבָרֵךְ יִרְאֵי יְיָ, הַקְּטַנִּים עִם הַגְּדֹלִים.

May the Eternal increase your numbers,
You and your children.
> Blessed are you by the Eternal,
> Maker of heaven and earth.

יֹסֵף יְיָ עֲלֵיכֶם,
עֲלֵיכֶם וְעַל בְּנֵיכֶם.
בְּרוּכִים אַתֶּם לַייָ, עֹשֵׂה שָׁמַיִם וָאָרֶץ.

The heavens are the heavens of the Eternal,
But the earth God gave to the children of men and women.
> The dead cannot praise the Eternal,
> Nor do any that sink into silence.

הַשָּׁמַיִם שָׁמַיִם לַייָ,
וְהָאָרֶץ נָתַן לִבְנֵי אָדָם.
לֹא הַמֵּתִים יְהַלְלוּ יָהּ,
וְלֹא כָּל יֹרְדֵי דוּמָה.

But we will bless the Eternal,
From this time forth and forever.
Halleluyah!

וַאֲנַחְנוּ נְבָרֵךְ יָהּ,
מֵעַתָּה וְעַד עוֹלָם, הַלְלוּיָהּ.

PSALM 116 *Responsive Reading*

I love the Eternal Who hears
My voice and my prayers.
> Because You turned Your ear to me,
> So shall I call upon You all my days.

אָהַבְתִּי כִּי יִשְׁמַע יְיָ,
אֶת קוֹלִי תַּחֲנוּנָי.
כִּי הִטָּה אָזְנוֹ לִי, וּבְיָמַי אֶקְרָא.

The bonds of death surrounded me,
And the terror of the grave seized me.
I was in anguish and despair.
> Then I called out Your name, Eternal,
> "O God, save my soul."

אֲפָפוּנִי חֶבְלֵי מָוֶת,
וּמְצָרֵי שְׁאוֹל מְצָאוּנִי,
צָרָה וְיָגוֹן אֶמְצָא.
וּבְשֵׁם יְיָ אֶקְרָא, אָנָּה יְיָ מַלְּטָה נַפְשִׁי.

Gracious and just is the Eternal.
Yes, our God is merciful.
> The Eternal guards the simple.
> I fell so low and You saved me

חַנּוּן יְיָ וְצַדִּיק,
וֵאלֹהֵינוּ מְרַחֵם.
שֹׁמֵר פְּתָאיִם יְיָ, דַּלּוֹתִי וְלִי יְהוֹשִׁיעַ.

Rest once again, O my soul,
For the Eternal has been good to you.
> For the Eternal has saved me from death,
>> My eyes from tears, my feet from stumbling.

I shall walk before the Eternal
In the land of the living.
> I had faith even when I cried out:
> "I suffer greatly."

And only in panic did I say:
"Every mortal is deceitful."
> How can I repay the Eternal,
> For all Your kindness to me?

I will lift up the cup of hope,
And call out the name of the Eternal.
> I will fulfill my vows to the Eternal,
> In the presence of all Your people.

Precious in the eyes of the Eternal,
Is the death of Your pious ones.
> O Eternal, truly I am Your servant;
> I am Your servant, born of Your servant;
> You have loosened my bonds.

I will bring You an offering of thanksgiving,
And will call upon the Eternal.
> I will fulfill my vows to the Eternal,
> In the presence of all Your people,
In the courts of the Eternal's house,
In the midst of Jerusalem. Halleluyah!

PSALM 117 RESPONSIVE READING

Let all nations praise the Eternal;
Let all peoples glorify God.
> For God's kindness for us is great;
> And the Eternal's truth is forever.
Halleluyah!

שׁוּבִי נַפְשִׁי לִמְנוּחָיְכִי,
כִּי יְיָ גָּמַל עָלָיְכִי.
כִּי חִלַּצְתָּ נַפְשִׁי מִמָּוֶת,
אֶת עֵינִי מִן דִּמְעָה, אֶת רַגְלִי מִדֶּחִי.

אֶתְהַלֵּךְ לִפְנֵי יְיָ,
בְּאַרְצוֹת הַחַיִּים.
הֶאֱמַנְתִּי כִּי אֲדַבֵּר, אֲנִי עָנִיתִי מְאֹד.

אֲנִי אָמַרְתִּי בְחָפְזִי,
כָּל הָאָדָם כֹּזֵב.
מָה אָשִׁיב לַיְיָ, כָּל תַּגְמוּלוֹהִי עָלָי.

כּוֹס יְשׁוּעוֹת אֶשָּׂא,
וּבְשֵׁם יְיָ אֶקְרָא.
נְדָרַי לַיְיָ אֲשַׁלֵּם, נֶגְדָה נָּא לְכָל עַמּוֹ.

יָקָר בְּעֵינֵי יְיָ,
הַמָּוְתָה לַחֲסִידָיו.
אָנָּה יְיָ, כִּי אֲנִי עַבְדֶּךָ,
אֲנִי עַבְדְּךָ בֶּן אֲמָתֶךָ, פִּתַּחְתָּ לְמוֹסֵרָי.

לְךָ אֶזְבַּח זֶבַח תּוֹדָה, וּבְשֵׁם יְיָ אֶקְרָא.
נְדָרַי לַיְיָ אֲשַׁלֵּם, נֶגְדָה נָּא לְכָל עַמּוֹ,
בְּחַצְרוֹת בֵּית יְיָ, בְּתוֹכֵכִי יְרוּשָׁלָיִם.
הַלְלוּיָהּ.

הַלְלוּ אֶת יְיָ, כָּל גּוֹיִם,
שַׁבְּחוּהוּ כָּל הָאֻמִּים.
כִּי גָבַר עָלֵינוּ חַסְדּוֹ, וֶאֱמֶת יְיָ לְעוֹלָם.
הַלְלוּיָהּ.

PSALM 118 *Responsive Reading*

Give thanks to the Eternal, Who is good,
Your love is eternal.
> Let Israel now say,
> That Your love is eternal.

Let the house of Aaron say,
That Your love is eternal.
> Let those who revere the Eternal say,
> That Your love is eternal.

Out of my distress I called upon the Eternal,
Who answered me and set me free.
> The Eternal is with me, I will not fear;
> What can mortals do to me?

The Eternal is with me as my helper;
I can overlook my enemies.
> It is better to trust in the Eternal
> Than to depend upon mortals.

It is better to trust in the Eternal
Than to depend upon nobility.
> Many nations encircled me;
> In the name of the Eternal,
> I overcame them.

They encircled me all around;
In the name of the Eternal,
I overcame them.
> They swarmed about me like bees;
> They dried up like thorns in a fire;
> In the name of the Eternal,
> I overcame them.

הוֹדוּ לַיְיָ כִּי טוֹב,
כִּי לְעוֹלָם חַסְדּוֹ.
יֹאמַר נָא יִשְׂרָאֵל,
כִּי לְעוֹלָם חַסְדּוֹ.

יֹאמְרוּ נָא בֵית אַהֲרֹן,
כִּי לְעוֹלָם חַסְדּוֹ.
יֹאמְרוּ נָא יִרְאֵי יְיָ,
כִּי לְעוֹלָם חַסְדּוֹ.

מִן הַמֵּצַר קָרָאתִי יָּהּ,
עָנָנִי בַמֶּרְחָב יָהּ.
יְיָ לִי לֹא אִירָא,
מַה יַּעֲשֶׂה לִי אָדָם.

יְיָ לִי בְּעֹזְרָי,
וַאֲנִי אֶרְאֶה בְשֹׂנְאָי.
טוֹב לַחֲסוֹת בַּיְיָ,
מִבְּטֹחַ בָּאָדָם.

טוֹב לַחֲסוֹת בַּיְיָ,
מִבְּטֹחַ בִּנְדִיבִים.
כָּל גּוֹיִם סְבָבוּנִי,
בְּשֵׁם יְיָ כִּי אֲמִילַם.

סַבּוּנִי גַם סְבָבוּנִי,
בְּשֵׁם יְיָ כִּי אֲמִילַם.
סַבּוּנִי כִדְבֹרִים,
דֹּעֲכוּ כְּאֵשׁ קוֹצִים,
בְּשֵׁם יְיָ כִּי אֲמִילַם.

They struck at me to make me fall;	דָּחֹה דְחִיתַנִי לִנְפֹּל,
But the Eternal helped me.	וַייָ עֲזָרָנִי.
The Eternal is my strength and my song,	עָזִּי וְזִמְרָת יָהּ,
And has become my salvation.	וַיְהִי לִי לִישׁוּעָה.
Hark! This joyous song of victory	קוֹל רִנָּה וִישׁוּעָה בְּאָהֳלֵי צַדִּיקִים:
Is heard in the tents of the righteous:	

"The right hand of the Eternal is valiant!	יְמִין יְיָ עֹשָׂה חָיִל.
The right hand of the Eternal is exalted!	יְמִין יְיָ רוֹמֵמָה.
The right hand of the Eternal is valiant!"	יְמִין יְיָ עֹשָׂה חָיִל.

I shall not die, but live	לֹא אָמוּת כִּי אֶחְיֶה,
To recount the works of the Eternal.	וַאֲסַפֵּר מַעֲשֵׂי יָהּ.
The Eternal punished me,	יַסֹּר יִסְּרַנִּי יָּהּ, וְלַמָּוֶת לֹא נְתָנָנִי.
But will not let me die.	

Open the gates of righteousness to me,	פִּתְחוּ לִי שַׁעֲרֵי צֶדֶק,
That I may enter and praise the Eternal.	אָבֹא בָם אוֹדֶה יָהּ.
This is the gate of the Eternal;	זֶה הַשַּׁעַר לַייָ, צַדִּיקִים יָבֹאוּ בוֹ.
The righteous alone shall enter.	

Directions: The leader(s) says each of the following verses; the participants repeat them.

I will give thanks unto You, for You have answered me,	אוֹדְךָ כִּי עֲנִיתָנִי,
And become my salvation. *(Repeat)*	וַתְּהִי לִי לִישׁוּעָה.
The stone which the builders rejected	אֶבֶן מָאֲסוּ הַבּוֹנִים,
Has become the chief cornerstone. *(Repeat)*	הָיְתָה לְרֹאשׁ פִּנָּה.

This is the work of the Eternal,	מֵאֵת יְיָ הָיְתָה זֹּאת,
It is marvelous in our eyes. *(Repeat)*	הִיא נִפְלָאת בְּעֵינֵינוּ.
This is the day that the Eternal has made;	זֶה הַיּוֹם עָשָׂה יְיָ,
Let us rejoice and be glad in it. *(Repeat)*	נָגִילָה וְנִשְׂמְחָה בוֹ.

We implore You, Eternal, save us! *(Repeat)*	אָנָּא יְיָ הוֹשִׁיעָה נָּא. *(Repeat)*
We implore You, Eternal, prosper us! *(Repeat)*	אָנָּא יְיָ הַצְלִיחָה נָּא. *(Repeat)*
Blessed are you who come in the name of the Eternal; *(Repeat)*	בָּרוּךְ הַבָּא בְּשֵׁם יְיָ, *(Repeat)*
We bless you from the house of the Eternal. *(Repeat)*	בֵּרַכְנוּכֶם מִבֵּית יְיָ. *(Repeat)*
The Eternal is God and has given us light;	אֵל יְיָ וַיָּאֶר לָנוּ, *(Repeat)*
Bind the offering with myrtle	אִסְרוּ חַג בַּעֲבֹתִים, *(Repeat)*
To the very corners of the altar. *(Repeat)*	עַד קַרְנוֹת הַמִּזְבֵּחַ. *(Repeat)*
You are my God, and I will give thanks to You;	אֵלִי אַתָּה וְאוֹדֶךָּ, *(Repeat)*
You are my God; I will extol You. *(Repeat)*	אֱלֹהַי אֲרוֹמְמֶךָּ. *(Repeat)*
Give thanks to the Eternal for You are good;	הוֹדוּ לַיְיָ כִּי טוֹב,
Your love is eternal. *(Repeat)*	כִּי לְעוֹלָם חַסְדּוֹ. *(Repeat)*

The Great Hallel   Psalm 136   הַלֵּל הַגָּדוֹל   *Responsive Reading*

Give thanks to the Eternal, Who is good, Your love is eternal. (Ki l'olam chasdo)	הוֹדוּ לַיְיָ כִּי טוֹב, כִּי לְעוֹלָם חַסְדּוֹ.
Give thanks to the God of gods, Your love is eternal.	הוֹדוּ לֵאלֹהֵי הָאֱלֹהִים, כִּי לְחַ.
Give thanks to the Ruler of rulers, Your love is eternal.	הוֹדוּ לַאֲדֹנֵי הָאֲדֹנִים, כִּי לְחַ.
Give thanks to You alone Who performs great wonders, Your love is eternal.	לְעֹשֵׂה נִפְלָאוֹת גְּדֹלוֹת לְבַדּוֹ, כִּי לְחַ.
Whose wisdom made the heavens, Your love is eternal.	לְעֹשֵׂה הַשָּׁמַיִם בִּתְבוּנָה, כִּי לְחַ.
Who spread the earth above the waters, Your love is eternal.	לְרוֹקַע הָאָרֶץ עַל הַמָּיִם, כִּי לְחַ.
And Who made the heavenly lights, Your love is eternal.	לְעֹשֵׂה אוֹרִים גְּדֹלִים, כִּי לְחַ.
The sun to rule by day, Your love is eternal.	אֶת הַשֶּׁמֶשׁ לְמֶמְשֶׁלֶת בַּיּוֹם, כִּי לְחַ.
The moon and the stars to rule by night, Your love is eternal.	אֶת הַיָּרֵחַ וְכוֹכָבִים לְמֶמְשְׁלוֹת בַּלָּיְלָה, כִּי לְחַ.

To You Who smote Egypt through their Firstborn,	כִּי לְעוֹלָם חַסְדּוֹ.	לְמַכֵּה מִצְרַיִם בִּבְכוֹרֵיהֶם,
Your love is eternal.	כִּי לְעוֹלָם חַסְדּוֹ.	וַיּוֹצֵא יִשְׂרָאֵל מִתּוֹכָם,
And brought Israel out of their midst,	כִּי לְעוֹלָם חַסְדּוֹ.	בְּיָד חֲזָקָה וּבִזְרוֹעַ נְטוּיָה,
Your love is eternal.	כִּי לְעוֹלָם חַסְדּוֹ.	לְגֹזֵר יַם סוּף לִגְזָרִים,
With a strong hand and outstretched arm,	כִּי לְעוֹלָם חַסְדּוֹ.	וְהֶעֱבִיר יִשְׂרָאֵל בְּתוֹכוֹ,
Your love is eternal.	כִּי לְעוֹלָם חַסְדּוֹ.	וְנִעֵר פַּרְעֹה וְחֵילוֹ בְיַם סוּף,
To You Who divided the Sea of Reeds,	כִּי לְעוֹלָם חַסְדּוֹ.	לְמוֹלִיךְ עַמּוֹ בַּמִּדְבָּר,
Your love is eternal.	כִּי לְעוֹלָם חַסְדּוֹ.	לְמַכֵּה מְלָכִים גְּדֹלִים,
And led Israel safely through it,	כִּי לְעוֹלָם חַסְדּוֹ.	וַיַּהֲרֹג מְלָכִים אַדִּירִים,
Your love is eternal.	כִּי לְעוֹלָם חַסְדּוֹ.	לְסִיחוֹן מֶלֶךְ הָאֱמֹרִי,
But overthrew Pharaoh and his army in the Sea of Reeds,	כִּי לְעוֹלָם חַסְדּוֹ.	וּלְעוֹג מֶלֶךְ הַבָּשָׁן,
Your love is eternal.	כִּי לְעוֹלָם חַסְדּוֹ.	וְנָתַן אַרְצָם לְנַחֲלָה,
To You Who led Your people through the wilderness,	כִּי לְעוֹלָם חַסְדּוֹ.	נַחֲלָה לְיִשְׂרָאֵל עַבְדּוֹ,
Your love is eternal.	כִּי לְעוֹלָם חַסְדּוֹ.	שֶׁבְּשִׁפְלֵנוּ זָכַר לָנוּ,
To You Who smote great kings,	כִּי לְעוֹלָם חַסְדּוֹ.	וַיִּפְרְקֵנוּ מִצָּרֵינוּ,
Your love is eternal.	כִּי לְעוֹלָם חַסְדּוֹ.	נוֹתֵן לֶחֶם לְכָל בָּשָׂר,
And struck down these mighty rulers,		הוֹדוּ לְאֵל הַשָּׁמַיִם,
Your love is eternal.		כִּי לְעוֹלָם חַסְדּוֹ.

Sichon, king of the Emorites,
    Your love is eternal.
And Og, king of Bashan,
    Your love is eternal.

And gave their land as a heritage,
    Your love is eternal.
A heritage to Israel, Your servant,
    Your love is eternal.
Who remembered us in our lowliness,
    Your love is eternal.
Who saved us from our enemies,
    Your love is eternal.
Who gives food to all creatures,
    Your love is eternal.
Give thanks to the God of heaven,
    for Your love is eternal.

Gratitude to God as the Sustainer   נִשְׁמַת   Nishmat

The soul of every living being shall bless Your name, Eternal our God; and the spirit of every creature shall glorify and extol Your fame, our Sovereign. From everlasting to everlasting, You are God, and only You save and help, Who free and rescue, support and have mercy in all times of trouble and distress. We have no Sovereign but You. O God of beginnings and endings, God of all creatures, Ruler of all generations, extolled with a multitude of praises, Who guides the world with loving kindness and Your creatures with tender mercy. God Who does not sleep or slumber awakens the sleeping and slumbering, gives voice to the speechless and frees the bound, supports the weak and raises the depressed, to You alone we give thanks.

נִשְׁמַת כָּל חַי, תְּבָרֵךְ אֶת שִׁמְךָ יְיָ אֱלֹהֵינוּ. וְרוּחַ כָּל בָּשָׂר תְּפָאֵר וּתְרוֹמֵם זִכְרְךָ מַלְכֵּנוּ תָּמִיד. מִן הָעוֹלָם וְעַד הָעוֹלָם אַתָּה אֵל וּמִבַּלְעָדֶיךָ אֵין לָנוּ מֶלֶךְ גּוֹאֵל וּמוֹשִׁיעַ, פּוֹדֶה וּמַצִּיל וּמְפַרְנֵס וּמְרַחֵם בְּכָל עֵת צָרָה וְצוּקָה. אֵין לָנוּ מֶלֶךְ אֶלָּא אַתָּה. אֱלֹהֵי הָרִאשׁוֹנִים וְהָאַחֲרוֹנִים, אֱלוֹהַּ כָּל בְּרִיּוֹת, אֲדוֹן כָּל תּוֹלָדוֹת, הַמְהֻלָּל בְּרֹב הַתִּשְׁבָּחוֹת, הַמְנַהֵג עוֹלָמוֹ בְּחֶסֶד וּבְרִיּוֹתָיו בְּרַחֲמִים. וַיְיָ לֹא יָנוּם וְלֹא יִישָׁן, הַמְעוֹרֵר יְשֵׁנִים וְהַמֵּקִיץ נִרְדָּמִים, וְהַמֵּשִׂיחַ אִלְּמִים, וְהַמַּתִּיר אֲסוּרִים, וְהַסּוֹמֵךְ נוֹפְלִים, וְהַזּוֹקֵף כְּפוּפִים, לְךָ לְבַדְּךָ אֲנַחְנוּ מוֹדִים.

If our mouths were filled with song as the sea, and our tongues with joy like its many waves; were our lips filled with praise as broad as the heaven, and our eyes shine with devotion as the sun and the moon; if our hands spread out in worship as the wings of eagles, and our feet could run as swiftly as deer; we would still be unable to thank You enough, Eternal our God and God of our ancestors, and to praise Your name for even the thousandth part—or even the millionth part—of all the goodness You bestowed upon our ancestors and upon us. For You redeemed us from Egypt, O Eternal our God, and freed us from the house of bondage.

אִלּוּ פִינוּ מָלֵא שִׁירָה כַּיָּם, וּלְשׁוֹנֵנוּ רִנָּה כַּהֲמוֹן גַּלָּיו, וְשִׂפְתוֹתֵינוּ שֶׁבַח כְּמֶרְחֲבֵי רָקִיעַ, וְעֵינֵינוּ מְאִירוֹת כַּשֶּׁמֶשׁ וְכַיָּרֵחַ, וְיָדֵינוּ פְרוּשׂוֹת כְּנִשְׁרֵי שָׁמָיִם, וְרַגְלֵינוּ קַלּוֹת כָּאַיָּלוֹת, אֵין אֲנַחְנוּ מַסְפִּיקִים, לְהוֹדוֹת לְךָ יְיָ אֱלֹהֵינוּ וֵאלֹהֵי אֲבוֹתֵינוּ, וּלְבָרֵךְ אֶת שִׁמְךָ עַל אַחַת מֵאֶלֶף אֶלֶף אַלְפֵי אֲלָפִים וְרִבֵּי רְבָבוֹת פְּעָמִים, הַטּוֹבוֹת שֶׁעָשִׂיתָ עִם אֲבוֹתֵינוּ וְעִמָּנוּ. מִמִּצְרַיִם גְּאַלְתָּנוּ יְיָ אֱלֹהֵינוּ וּמִבֵּית עֲבָדִים פְּדִיתָנוּ.

בָּרָעָב זַנְתָּנוּ, וּבְשָׂבָע כִּלְכַּלְתָּנוּ, מֵחֶרֶב הִצַּלְתָּנוּ, וּמִדֶּבֶר מִלַּטְתָּנוּ, וּמֵחֳלָיִם רָעִים וְנֶאֱמָנִים דִּלִּיתָנוּ. עַד הֵנָּה עֲזָרוּנוּ רַחֲמֶיךָ, וְלֹא עֲזָבוּנוּ חֲסָדֶיךָ וְאַל תִּטְּשֵׁנוּ יְיָ אֱלֹהֵינוּ לָנֶצַח.

You fed us when we were hungry and sustained us in plenty. You saved us from the sword, rescued us from the plague, and spared us serious illnesses. Until now, Your tender mercy has helped us, and Your kindness has not failed us. Do not forsake us ever, Eternal our God.

עַל כֵּן אֵבָרִים שֶׁפִּלַּגְתָּ בָּנוּ, וְרוּחַ וּנְשָׁמָה שֶׁנָּפַחְתָּ בְּאַפֵּינוּ, וְלָשׁוֹן אֲשֶׁר שַׂמְתָּ בְּפִינוּ, הֵן הֵם יוֹדוּ וִיבָרְכוּ וִישַׁבְּחוּ וִיפָאֲרוּ וִירוֹמְמוּ וְיַעֲרִיצוּ וְיַקְדִּישׁוּ וְיַמְלִיכוּ אֶת שִׁמְךָ מַלְכֵּנוּ. כִּי כָל פֶּה לְךָ יוֹדֶה, וְכָל לָשׁוֹן לְךָ תִשָּׁבַע, וְכָל בֶּרֶךְ לְךָ תִכְרַע, וְכָל קוֹמָה לְפָנֶיךָ תִשְׁתַּחֲוֶה, וְכָל לְבָבוֹת יִירָאוּךָ, וְכָל קֶרֶב וּכְלָיוֹת יְזַמְּרוּ לִשְׁמֶךָ. כַּדָּבָר שֶׁכָּתוּב, כָּל עַצְמוֹתַי תֹּאמַרְנָה

Therefore, the limbs You formed in us, and the spirit of life You breathed into our nostrils, and the tongue You placed in our mouths—all join to thank, praise, bless, glorify, exalt, adore, extol, revere, hallow and give sovereignty to Your name. For every mouth shall give thanks to You, and every tongue shall declare allegiance to You; and every knee shall bend to You, and every living being shall kneel before You; all hearts shall revere You, and every person's inner self shall sing praises to Your name, as it is written: "All my bones shall say, Eternal,

יְיָ מִי כָמוֹךָ. מַצִּיל עָנִי מֵחָזָק מִמֶּנּוּ, וְעָנִי וְאֶבְיוֹן מִגֹּזְלוֹ.

Who is like You? You deliver the weak from those who are stronger, the poor and needy from those who would rob them."
(Psalms 35:10)

מִי יִדְמֶה לָּךְ, וּמִי יִשְׁוֶה לָּךְ וּמִי יַעֲרָךְ לָךְ. הָאֵל הַגָּדוֹל הַגִּבּוֹר וְהַנּוֹרָא אֵל עֶלְיוֹן קֹנֵה שָׁמַיִם וָאָרֶץ. נְהַלֶּלְךָ וּנְשַׁבֵּחֲךָ וּנְפָאֶרְךָ וּנְבָרֵךְ אֶת שֵׁם קָדְשֶׁךָ, כָּאָמוּר, לְדָוִד, בָּרְכִי נַפְשִׁי אֶת יְיָ, וְכָל קְרָבַי אֶת שֵׁם קָדְשׁוֹ.

Who is like You, and who can equal You? Who can compare with You, O great, mighty, revered and supreme God, Owner of heaven and earth? Let us praise, acclaim, glorify and bless Your holy Name in the words of the Psalm of David: "Bless the Eternal, O my soul, and all that is within me, bless God's Holy Name!" *(103:1)*

הָאֵל בְּתַעֲצֻמוֹת עֻזֶּךָ, הַגָּדוֹל בִּכְבוֹד שְׁמֶךָ, הַגִּבּוֹר לָנֶצַח וְהַנּוֹרָא בְּנוֹרְאוֹתֶיךָ, הַמֶּלֶךְ הַיּוֹשֵׁב עַל כִּסֵּא רָם וְנִשָּׂא.

You are God by the power of Your might, great by the glory of Your Name, mighty forever, revered for Your awe-inspiring deeds; You are the Ruler enthroned on high and exalted.

You Who dwell in eternity, exalted and holy is Your Name. As it is written: "Rejoice in the Eternal, you who are righteous ones; it is fitting for the upright to praise God." *(33:1)* By the mouth of the upright, You shall be praised! By the words of the righteous, You shall be blessed! By the tongue of the pious, You shall be exalted! And in the midst of the holy, You shall be sanctified.

שׁוֹכֵן עַד, מָרוֹם וְקָדוֹשׁ שְׁמוֹ. וְכָתוּב, רַנְּנוּ צַדִּיקִים בַּיְיָ, לַיְשָׁרִים נָאוָה תְהִלָּה. בְּפִי יְשָׁרִים תִּתְהַלָּל, וּבְדִבְרֵי צַדִּיקִים תִּתְבָּרַךְ, וּבִלְשׁוֹן חֲסִידִים תִּתְרוֹמָם, וּבְקֶרֶב קְדוֹשִׁים תִּתְקַדָּשׁ.

In the assembled multitudes of Your people, the House of Israel, Your Name, O our Ruler, shall be glorified with song in every generation. For it is the duty of all creatures in Your presence, O Eternal our God, and God of our ancestors, to thank, praise, glorify, honor, revere, bless, exalt and adore You even beyond all the words of song and praise uttered by David, son of Jesse, Your anointed servant.

וּבְמַקְהֲלוֹת רִבְבוֹת עַמְּךָ בֵּית יִשְׂרָאֵל בְּרִנָּה יִתְפָּאֵר שִׁמְךָ מַלְכֵּנוּ, בְּכָל דּוֹר וָדוֹר, שֶׁכֵּן חוֹבַת כָּל הַיְצוּרִים לְפָנֶיךָ, יְיָ אֱלֹהֵינוּ וֵאלֹהֵי אֲבוֹתֵינוּ, לְהוֹדוֹת לְהַלֵּל לְשַׁבֵּחַ לְפָאֵר לְרוֹמֵם לְהַדֵּר לְבָרֵךְ לְעַלֵּה וּלְקַלֵּס עַל כָּל דִּבְרֵי שִׁירוֹת וְתִשְׁבָּחוֹת דָּוִד בֶּן יִשַׁי עַבְדְּךָ מְשִׁיחֶךָ.

Praised be Your Name forever, our Sovereign, the great and holy God and Ruler in heaven and earth. For to You, Eternal our God and God of our ancestors are due song and praise, hymn and psalm acclaiming Your strength and dominion, victory and glory, holiness and sovereignty

יִשְׁתַּבַּח שִׁמְךָ לָעַד מַלְכֵּנוּ, הָאֵל הַמֶּלֶךְ הַגָּדוֹל וְהַקָּדוֹשׁ בַּשָּׁמַיִם וּבָאָרֶץ. כִּי לְךָ נָאֶה, יְיָ אֱלֹהֵינוּ וֵאלֹהֵי אֲבוֹתֵינוּ, שִׁיר וּשְׁבָחָה, הַלֵּל וְזִמְרָה, עֹז וּמֶמְשָׁלָה, נֶצַח, גְּדֻלָּה וּגְבוּרָה, תְּהִלָּה וְתִפְאֶרֶת, קְדֻשָּׁה וּמַלְכוּת,

To You we offer blessings and thanksgiving from this time forth and forever.

בְּרָכוֹת וְהוֹדָאוֹת מֵעַתָּה וְעַד עוֹלָם.

All Your works shall praise You, Eternal our God. Your pious righteous servants who do Your will as well as all Your people, the House of Israel, will joyfully thank, bless, praise, glorify, exalt, revere, sanctify and proclaim the sovereignty of Your Name, our Ruler.

יְהַלְלוּךָ יְיָ אֱלֹהֵינוּ כָּל מַעֲשֶׂיךָ וַחֲסִידֶיךָ צַדִּיקִים עוֹשֵׂי רְצוֹנֶךָ, וְכָל עַמְּךָ בֵּית יִשְׂרָאֵל בְּרִנָּה יוֹדוּ וִיבָרְכוּ וִישַׁבְּחוּ וִיפָאֲרוּ וִירוֹמְמוּ וְיַעֲרִיצוּ וְיַקְדִּישׁוּ וְיַמְלִיכוּ אֶת שִׁמְךָ מַלְכֵּנוּ.

It is good to give thanks to You and fitting to sing praises to Your Name, for You are God from this world to the next. Blessed are You, Eternal, Ruler glorified in praises.

כִּי לְךָ טוֹב לְהוֹדוֹת וּלְשִׁמְךָ נָאֶה לְזַמֵּר, כִּי מֵעוֹלָם וְעַד עוֹלָם אַתָּה אֵל. בָּרוּךְ אַתָּה יְיָ, מֶלֶךְ מְהֻלָּל בַּתִּשְׁבָּחוֹת.

Directions: Leader(s) raises the fourth cup of wine as all say:

Baruch Ata Adonai, Eloheinu Melech ha-olam, borei p'ri hagafen.

בָּרוּךְ אַתָּה יְיָ אֱלֹהֵינוּ מֶלֶךְ הָעוֹלָם, בּוֹרֵא פְּרִי הַגָּפֶן.

Blessed are You, Eternal our God, Ruler of the universe, Who creates the fruit of the vine.

Directions: Drink the fourth cup of wine while reclining to the left.

Blessed are You, Eternal our God, Ruler of the universe, for the fruit of the vine; for the produce of the field and for the desirable, good and spacious land which You gave, in favor, to our ancestors, as a heritage, that they might eat its fruits and enjoy its bounty. Have compassion, O Eternal our God, on Israel Your people, on Jerusalem Your City, on Zion, the dwelling place of Your glory, on Your altar and on Your Temple. Rebuild Jerusalem, Your holy City, speedily in our days. Bring us there and let us rejoice in its rebuilding, that we may eat its fruits and enjoy its goodness so that we may bless You there in holiness and purity. (On the Sabbath add: May it please You to strengthen us on this Sabbath day.) Let us rejoice on this Festival of Unleavened Bread. For You, O God, are good and charitable to all and we thank You for the land and the fruit of the vine. Blessed are You, Eternal, for the land and the fruit of the vine.

בָּרוּךְ אַתָּה יְיָ אֱלֹהֵינוּ מֶלֶךְ הָעוֹלָם עַל הַגֶּפֶן וְעַל פְּרִי הַגֶּפֶן, וְעַל תְּנוּבַת הַשָּׂדֶה, וְעַל אֶרֶץ חֶמְדָּה טוֹבָה וּרְחָבָה שֶׁרָצִיתָ וְהִנְחַלְתָּ לַאֲבוֹתֵינוּ, לֶאֱכוֹל מִפִּרְיָהּ וְלִשְׂבּוֹעַ מִטּוּבָהּ. רַחֶם נָא יְיָ אֱלֹהֵינוּ עַל יִשְׂרָאֵל עַמֶּךָ, וְעַל יְרוּשָׁלַיִם עִירֶךָ, וְעַל צִיּוֹן מִשְׁכַּן כְּבוֹדֶךָ, וְעַל מִזְבְּחֶךָ וְעַל הֵיכָלֶךָ. וּבְנֵה יְרוּשָׁלַיִם עִיר הַקֹּדֶשׁ בִּמְהֵרָה בְיָמֵינוּ, וְהַעֲלֵנוּ לְתוֹכָהּ, וְשַׂמְּחֵנוּ בְּבִנְיָנָהּ וְנֹאכַל מִפִּרְיָהּ וְנִשְׂבַּע מִטּוּבָהּ, וּנְבָרֶכְךָ עָלֶיהָ בִּקְדֻשָּׁה וּבְטָהֳרָה. (בשבת וּרְצֵה וְהַחֲלִיצֵנוּ בְּיוֹם הַשַּׁבָּת הַזֶּה.) וְשַׂמְּחֵנוּ בְּיוֹם חַג הַמַּצּוֹת הַזֶּה. כִּי אַתָּה יְיָ טוֹב וּמֵטִיב לַכֹּל, וְנוֹדֶה לְּךָ עַל הָאָרֶץ וְעַל פְּרִי הַגָּפֶן. בָּרוּךְ אַתָּה יְיָ, עַל הָאָרֶץ וְעַל פְּרִי הַגָּפֶן.

14. Nirtzah   נִרְצָה   Conclude the Seder

This poem, which concludes the formal part of the Seder, originated in Southern France almost one thousand years ago.

חֲסַל סִדּוּר פֶּסַח כְּהִלְכָתוֹ, כְּכָל
מִשְׁפָּטוֹ וְחֻקָּתוֹ. כַּאֲשֶׁר זָכִינוּ
לְסַדֵּר אוֹתוֹ, כֵּן נִזְכֶּה לַעֲשׂוֹתוֹ.
זָךְ שׁוֹכֵן מְעוֹנָה, קוֹמֵם קְהַל
עֲדַת מִי מָנָה. בְּקָרוֹב נַהֵל
נִטְעֵי כַנָּה, פְּדוּיִים לְצִיּוֹן בְּרִנָּה.

Our Seder is now concluded,
Each custom and law fulfilled.
Just as we were worthy to celebrate it tonight,
may we be worthy to do so in future years.
O Pure One, Who dwells on high, raise up Your numberless people! Speedily lead the shoots of Your stock redeemed, to Zion with joyous song.

L'shana Haba-a Bi'rushala'yim Hab'nuyah!

לְשָׁנָה הַבָּאָה בִּירוּשָׁלַיִם הַבְּנוּיָה.

May Israel forever strive to be a beacon of justice, mercy and truth in the world. May the coming year bring freedom to the oppressed, peace to Zion and Jerusalem, and witness the redemption of Israel. "For out of Zion shall go forth the Torah, and the word of God from Jerusalem." *(Is. 2:3)*

"NEXT YEAR IN REBUILT JERUSALEM!"

FOR THE FIRST SEDER NIGHT ONLY

This poem, in alphabetical acrostic, is probably from the seventh century. It enumerates many miracles in Biblical history and concludes with the hope of ultimate redemption.

And It Came to Pass at Midnight   "וּבְכֵן וַיְהִי בַּחֲצִי הַלַּיְלָה"

In olden days, You performed many miracles at night. At the beginning of the watches on this night, Abraham gained victory by dividing his army at night. *(Gen. 14:15)*

בְּרֹאשׁ אַשְׁמוּרוֹת זֶה הַלַּיְלָה, גֵּר צֶדֶק נִצַּחְתּוֹ כְּנֶחֱלַק לוֹ לַיְלָה. אָז רוֹב נִסִּים הִפְלֵאתָ בַּלַּיְלָה.

    And it came to pass at midnight.,

וַיְהִי בַּחֲצִי הַלַּיְלָה.

You judged Abimelech, king of Gerar, in a dream during the night. *(Gen. 20:3)* You struck Laban, the Syrian, with terror in the night. *(Gen. 31:24)* Israel wrestled with an angel and prevailed at night. *(Gen. 32:25)*

דַּנְתָּ מֶלֶךְ גְּרָר בַּחֲלוֹם הַלַּיְלָה, הִפְחַדְתָּ אֲרַמִּי בְּאֶמֶשׁ לַיְלָה, וַיָּשַׂר יִשְׂרָאֵל לְמַלְאָךְ וַיּוּכַל לוֹ לַיְלָה.

    And it came to pass at midnight.

וַיְהִי בַּחֲצִי הַלַּיְלָה.

You struck down Pathros' (Egypt's) firstborn at night. *(Ex. 12:29)* The Egyptians were without wealth when they arose at night. You scattered Sissera's army, aided by the stars at night. *(Judg. 5:20)*

זֶרַע בְּכוֹרֵי פַתְרוֹס מָחַצְתָּ בַּחֲצִי הַלַּיְלָה, חֵילָם לֹא מָצְאוּ בְּקוּמָם בַּלַּיְלָה, טִיסַת נְגִיד חֲרוֹשֶׁת סִלִּיתָ בְּכוֹכְבֵי לָיְלָה.

    It came to pass at midnight.

וַיְהִי בַּחֲצִי הַלַּיְלָה.

The Assyrian army was decimated at night. *(2 Ki. 19:35)* Babylonia's god, Bel, and his pedestal crashed in the night. *(Is. 46:1,2)* Mysteries were revealed to Daniel in a vision at night. *(Dan. 2:19)*

יָעַץ מְחָרֵף לְנוֹפֵף אִוּוּי הוֹבַשְׁתָּ פְגָרָיו בַּלַּיְלָה, כָּרַע בֵּל וּמַצָּבוֹ בְּאִישׁוֹן לַיְלָה, לְאִישׁ חֲמוּדוֹת נִגְלָה רָז חֲזוֹת לַיְלָה.

    It came to pass at midnight.

וַיְהִי בַּחֲצִי הַלַּיְלָה.

Drunken Belshazzar was slain at night. *(Dan. 5:30)* Daniel, saved from the lions' den, interpreted the dreams of night. *(Dan. 6:24)* Hateful Haman wrote his edicts at night. *(Esth. 3:12)*

It came to pass at midnight.

You triumphed over Haman when sleep failed Ahasuerus at night. *(Esth. 6:1)* You will tread the winepress for those who ask: "Watchman, what of the night?" *(Is. 6:3, 21:11)* Like the watchman, you will answer: "Morning comes even as the night." *(Is. 21:12)*

It came to pass at midnight.

Hasten that day which is not day nor night. *(Zech. 14:7)* Most High, proclaim that Yours is day, and Yours is also night. Place guards to watch the city, day and night. *(Is. 62:6)* Make bright as day the darkness of the night.

May it come to pass at midnight.

מִשְׁתַּכֵּר בִּכְלֵי קֹדֶשׁ נֶהֱרַג בּוֹ בַּלַּיְלָה, נוֹשַׁע מִבּוֹר אֲרָיוֹת פּוֹתֵר בְּעִתּוּתֵי לַיְלָה. שִׂנְאָה נָטַר אֲגָגִי וְכָתַב סְפָרִים לַיְלָה.

וַיְהִי בַּחֲצִי הַלַּיְלָה.

עוֹרַרְתָּ נִצְחֲךָ עָלָיו בְּנֶדֶד שְׁנַת לַיְלָה, פּוּרָה תִדְרוֹךְ לְשׁוֹמֵר מַה מִּלַּיְלָה, צָרַח כַּשּׁוֹמֵר וְשָׂח אָתָא בֹקֶר וְגַם לָיְלָה.

וַיְהִי בַּחֲצִי הַלַּיְלָה.

קָרֵב יוֹם אֲשֶׁר הוּא לֹא יוֹם וְלֹא לַיְלָה, רָם הוֹדַע כִּי לְךָ הַיּוֹם אַף לְךָ הַלַּיְלָה, שׁוֹמְרִים הַפְקֵד לְעִירְךָ כָּל הַיּוֹם וְכָל הַלַּיְלָה, תָּאִיר כְּאוֹר יוֹם חֶשְׁכַּת לָיְלָה.

הִי בַּחֲצִי הַלַּיְלָה.

FOR THE SECOND SEDER NIGHT ONLY

In alphabetical acrostic with events in chronological order, this eighth century poem tells of how God repeatedly rescued us during the Passover season.

And You Shall Say: This Is the Feast of Passover. וּבְכֵן וַאֲמַרְתֶּם זֶבַח פֶּסַח

Your mighty power You revealed on Passover; above all the festivals You exalted Passover; to Abraham and Sarah You revealed the midnight marvels of Passover. *(Baba Bathra 15a)*

אֹמֶץ גְּבוּרוֹתֶיךָ הִפְלֵאתָ בַּפֶּסַח,
בְּרֹאשׁ כָּל מוֹעֲדוֹת נִשֵּׂאתָ פֶּסַח,
גִּלִּיתָ לְאֶזְרָחִי חֲצוֹת לֵיל פֶּסַח.

    This is the feast of Passover.   וַאֲמַרְתֶּם זֶבַח פֶּסַח.

To Abraham and Sarah's door You came at midday's heat on Passover; they served the angels with unleavened bread on Passover; and to the herd Abraham ran, to fetch a calf for Passover. *(Gen. 18:1,6,7)*

דְּלָתָיו דָּפַקְתָּ כְּחֹם הַיּוֹם בַּפֶּסַח,
הִסְעִיד נוֹצְצִים עֻגוֹת מַצּוֹת בַּפֶּסַח,
וְאֶל הַבָּקָר רָץ זֵכֶר לְשׁוֹר עֵרֶךְ פֶּסַח.

    This is the feast of Passover.   אֲמַרְתֶּם זֶבַח פֶּסַח.

The Sodomites angered God and were consumed by fire on Passover. But Lot was saved, and baked unleavened bread on Passover. *(Gen. 19:3)* You swept away the power of Egypt on Passover.

זֹעֲמוּ סְדוֹמִים וְלֹהֲטוּ בָאֵשׁ בַּפֶּסַח,
חֻלַּץ לוֹט מֵהֶם וּמַצּוֹת אָפָה בְּקֵץ פֶּסַח,
טִאטֵאתָ אַדְמַת מוֹף וְנוֹף בְּעָבְרְךָ בַּפֶּסַח.

    This is the feast of Passover.   וַאֲמַרְתֶּם זֶבַח פֶּסַח.

You, God, demolished the firstborn of Egypt on the night of Passover. O Mighty One, You spared Israel, Your Firstborn on Passover. Death passed over Israel's marked doors on Passover. *(Ex. 12:23)*

יָהּ רֹאשׁ כָּל אוֹן מָחַצְתָּ בְּלֵיל שִׁמּוּר פֶּסַח,
כַּבִּיר, עַל בֵּן בְּכוֹר פָּסַחְתָּ בְּדַם פֶּסַח,
לְבִלְתִּי תֵּת מַשְׁחִית לָבֹא בִּפְתָחַי בַּפֶּסַח.

    This is the feast of Passover.   וַאֲמַרְתֶּם זֶבַח פֶּסַח.

The walled city of Jericho fell on Passover. *(Josh. 6:5)* Through a dream of barley loaf, Midian was destroyed on Passover. *(Judg. 7:13)* The mighty Assyrian hordes were consumed in blazing flame on Passover. *(Midrash Yal. Shim.)*

 This is the feast of Passover.

Sennecherib met disaster at Zion's gate on Passover. *(Is. 10:32)* A hand wrote Babylonia's fate upon a wall on Passover. *(Dan. 5:24)* "The watch is set; the table is spread." *(Is. 21:5)* Feasting Babylonia merits doom on Passover.

 This is the feast of Passover.

Queen Esther gathered the community for a three-day fast on Passover. *(Esth. 4:16)* The wicked Haman was hung on gallows fifty cubits high on Passover. *(Esth. 7:9)* A double punishment shall You bring upon our foes on Passover. *(Is. 47:9)* Your hand is strong, Your right hand uplifted, Your might shall again prevail on Passover. *(Ps. 89:14)*

 This is the feast of Passover.

מִסְגֶּרֶת סֻגָּרָה בְּעִתּוֹתֵי פֶּסַח, נִשְׁמְדָה מִדְיָן בִּצְלִיל שְׂעוֹרֵי עֹמֶר פֶּסַח, שֹׂרְפוּ מִשְׁמַנֵּי פּוּל וְלוּד בִּיקַד יְקוֹד פֶּסַח.

וַאֲמַרְתֶּם זֶבַח פֶּסַח.

עוֹד הַיּוֹם בְּנֹב לַעֲמוֹד עַד גָּעָה עוֹנַת פֶּסַח, פַּס יָד כָּתְבָה לְקַעֲקֵעַ צוּל בַּפֶּסַח, צָפֹה הַצָּפִית עָרוֹךְ הַשֻּׁלְחָן, בַּפֶּסַח.

וַאֲמַרְתֶּם זֶבַח פֶּסַח.

קָהָל כִּנְּסָה הֲדַסָּה צוֹם לְשַׁלֵּשׁ בַּפֶּסַח, רֹאשׁ מִבֵּית רָשָׁע מָחַצְתָּ בְּעֵץ חֲמִשִּׁים בַּפֶּסַח, שְׁתֵּי אֵלֶּה רֶגַע, תָּבִיא לְעוּצִית בַּפֶּסַח, תָּעֹז יָדְךָ וְתָרוּם יְמִינֶךָ, כְּלֵיל הִתְקַדֶּשׁ חַג פֶּסַח.

וַאֲמַרְתֶּם זֶבַח פֶּסַח.

The Counting of Omer   סְפִירָה   S'firah

Directions: To be recited beginning with the second night.

According to ancient custom, a measure *(omer)* of the new barley harvest was brought to the Temple each year to begin the counting of the fifty days between the second night of Passover and *Shavuot* (the festival that celebrates the giving of the Torah). *(Lev. 23:10,15,16; Deut. 16:9)* The Israelites were told that fifty days after the Exodus, when their souls were purified, they would receive the Torah on Mount Sinai. In eager anticipation, they counted off the days until the event occurred. By continuing the tradition, we closely link the Exodus (Passover) with the giving of the Torah *(Shavuot)* and freedom from slavery to the Pharaoh to freedom in serving God.

I am ready to fulfill the mitzvah of counting the Omer, as it is written in the Torah: "You shall count from the night of the second day of Passover, when you bring an Omer of grain as an offering, seven complete weeks. The day after the seventh week of your counting will make fifty days" *(Leviticus 23:15-16)*.

הִנְנִי מוּכָן וּמְזֻמָּן לְקַיֵּם מִצְוַת עֲשֵׂה שֶׁל סְפִירַת הָעֹמֶר, כְּמוֹ שֶׁכָּתוּב בַּתּוֹרָה: וּסְפַרְתֶּם לָכֶם מִמָּחֳרַת הַשַּׁבָּת, מִיּוֹם הֲבִיאֲכֶם אֶת עֹמֶר הַתְּנוּפָה שֶׁבַע שַׁבָּתוֹת תְּמִימֹת תִּהְיֶינָה, עַד מִמָּחֳרַת הַשַּׁבָּת הַשְּׁבִיעִית תִּסְפְּרוּ חֲמִשִּׁים יוֹם.

Blessed are You, Eternal our God, Ruler of the universe, Who has sanctified us with Your commandments and instructed us to count the **Omer**.

בָּרוּךְ אַתָּה יְיָ אֱלֹהֵינוּ מֶלֶךְ הָעוֹלָם, אֲשֶׁר קִדְּשָׁנוּ בְּמִצְוֹתָיו וְצִוָּנוּ עַל סְפִירַת הָעֹמֶר.

This is the first day of the **Omer**.

הַיּוֹם יוֹם אֶחָד לָעֹמֶר.

Over the years, new songs were added to the end of the Seder, many of which were especially appealing to the children. Let us join together and sing these rousing and spirited melodies that have come to be cherished in the Haggadah.

To You Praise Is Proper   כִּי לוֹ נָאֶה   Ki lo na-eh

The theme of Ki lo na-eh, written in alphabetical acrostic from the fifteenth century, is the mysterious combination of God's love, sovereignty, power and gentleness.

Ki lo na-eh;   כִּי לוֹ נָאֶה,
Ki lo ya-eh.   כִּי לוֹ יָאֶה.

To You praise is proper;
To You praise is due.

Adir bim'lucha, Bachur ka-halacha,   אַדִּיר בִּמְלוּכָה, בָּחוּר כַּהֲלָכָה,
G'dudav yom'ru lo: גְּדוּדָיו יֹאמְרוּ לוֹ:

*Chorus:** L'cha u-l'cha, L'cha ki l'cha, L'cha af l'cha, L'cha Adonai hamam'lacha.   *לְךָ וּלְךָ, לְךָ כִּי לְךָ, לְךָ אַף לְךָ, לְךָ יְיָ הַמַּמְלָכָה.

Ki lo na-eh; Ki lo ya-eh.   כִּי לוֹ נָאֶה, כִּי לוֹ יָאֶה.

         Mighty in Majesty, truly Distinguished,
            Your host of angels sing to You:
        ***Chorus:** *To You truly, To You alone,*
     To You only, To You, O God, is the sovereignty.
       To You praise is proper; to You praise is due.

Da-gul bim'lucha, Hadur ka-halacha,   דָּגוּל בִּמְלוּכָה, הָדוּר כַּהֲלָכָה, וְתִיקָיו
V'tikav yom'ru lo: יֹאמְרוּ לוֹ:

*Chorus:** L'cha u-l'cha, L'cha ki l'cha, L'cha af l'cha, L'cha Adonai hamam'lacha.   *לְךָ וּלְךָ, לְךָ כִּי לְךָ, לְךָ אַף לְךָ, לְךָ יְיָ הַמַּמְלָכָה.
Ki lo-na-eh; Ki lo ya-eh.   כִּי לוֹ נָאֶה, כִּי לוֹ יָאֶה.

            First in Majesty, truly glorious,
              Your faithful sing to You:
        ***Chorus:** *To You truly, To You alone,*
     To You only, To You, O God, is the sovereignty.
       To You praise is proper; to You praise is due.

Zakai bim'lucha, Chasin ka-halacha, Taf's'rav yom'ru lo: *(Repeat Chorus)

זַכַּאי בִּמְלוּכָה, חָסִין כַּהֲלָכָה, טַפְסְרָיו יֹאמְרוּ לוֹ:*

    Just in Majesty, truly powerful,
    Your subjects sing to You: *(Repeat Chorus)*

Yachid bim'lucha, Kabir ka-halacha, Limudav yom'ru lo: *(Repeat Chorus)

יָחִיד בִּמְלוּכָה, כַּבִּיר כַּהֲלָכָה, לִמּוּדָיו יֹאמְרוּ לוֹ:*

    Unique in Majesty, truly grand,
    Your disciples sing to You: *(Repeat Chorus)*

Moshel bim'lucha, Nora ka-halacha, S'vivav yom'ru lo: *(Repeat Chorus)

מוֹשֵׁל בִּמְלוּכָה, נוֹרָא כַּהֲלָכָה, סְבִיבָיו יֹאמְרוּ לוֹ:*

    Ruler in Majesty, truly revered,
    Your angels sing to You: *(Repeat Chorus)*

Anav bim'lucha, Podeh ka-halacha, Tzadikav yom'ru lo: *(Repeat Chorus)

עָנָו בִּמְלוּכָה, פּוֹדֶה כַּהֲלָכָה, צַדִּיקָיו יֹאמְרוּ לוֹ:*

    Humble in Majesty, truly redeeming,
    Your righteous sing to You: *(Repeat Chorus)*

Kadosh bim'lucha, Rachum ka-halacha, Shin'anav yom'ru lo: *(Repeat Chorus)

קָדוֹשׁ בִּמְלוּכָה, רַחוּם כַּהֲלָכָה, שִׁנְאַנָּיו יֹאמְרוּ לוֹ:*

    Holy in Majesty, truly merciful,
    Your worshippers sing to You: *(Repeat Chorus)*

Takif bim'lucha, Tomech ka-halacha, T'mimav yom'ru lo:

תַּקִּיף בִּמְלוּכָה, תּוֹמֵךְ כַּהֲלָכָה, תְּמִימָיו יֹאמְרוּ לוֹ:

Chorus: * L'cha u-l'cha, L'cha ki l'cha, L'cha af l'cha, L'cha Adonai hamam'lacha. Ki lo-na-eh; Ki lo ya-eh.

*לְךָ וּלְךָ, לְךָ כִּי לְךָ, לְךָ אַף לְךָ, לְךָ יְיָ הַמַּמְלָכָה. כִּי לוֹ נָאֶה, כִּי לוֹ יָאֶה.

    Determined in Majesty, truly supportive,
    Your upright sing to You:

    Chorus: *To You truly, To You alone,
    To You only, To You, O God, is the sovereignty.
    To You praise is proper; to You praise is due.

Mighty Are You! אַדִיר הוּא Adir Hu

Of unknown authorship, this popular song expresses hope for the speedy rebuilding of the Temple. The word "Temple" here refers to the land of Israel as the religious center of the Jewish people.

Adir Hu! Adir Hu!   אַדִיר הוּא, אַדִיר הוּא,
Chorus: *Yiv'neh vei-to b'karov.   *יִבְנֶה בֵיתוֹ בְּקָרוֹב,
Bim'hera, bim'hera,   בִּמְהֵרָה בִּמְהֵרָה, בְּיָמֵינוּ בְּקָרוֹב.
B'yameinu b'karov.
El B'neh! El B'neh!   אֵל בְּנֵה, אֵל בְּנֵה,
B'neh veit'cha b'karov.   בְּנֵה בֵיתְךָ בְּקָרוֹב.

         Mighty One! Mighty One!
         Chorus: *May You rebuild Your Temple.
    Speedily, speedily, in our lifetime quickly.
          O God, rebuild! O God, rebuild!
           Rebuild Your Temple soon.

Bachur Hu, gadol Hu, dagul Hu!   *בָּחוּר הוּא, גָּדוֹל הוּא, דָּגוּל הוּא,
*(Repeat Chorus)

     Chosen, great, renowned are You! *(Repeat Chorus)

Hadur Hu, vatik Hu, zakai Hu,   הָדוּר הוּא, וָתִיק הוּא, זַכַּאי הוּא,
chasid Hu! *(Repeat Chorus)   חָסִיד הוּא,*

  Glorious, distinguished, faultless and gracious are You! *(Repeat Chorus)

Tahor Hu, yachid Hu, ka-bir Hu,   טָהוֹר הוּא, יָחִיד הוּא, כַּבִּיר הוּא,
la-mud Hu, Melech hu, no-rah Hu,   לָמוּד הוּא, מֶלֶךְ הוּא, נוֹרָא הוּא,
sa-giv Hu, izuz Hu, podeh Hu,   סַגִּיב הוּא, עִזּוּז הוּא, פּוֹדֶה הוּא,
tzadik Hu,! *(Repeat Chorus)   צַדִּיק הוּא,*

  Pure, unique, mighty, wise, majestic, revered, exalted, invincible, redeeming and
                 righteous are You!* (Repeat Chorus)

Kadosh Hu, rachum Hu, shadai hu, takif   קָדוֹשׁ הוּא, רַחוּם הוּא, שַׁדַּי הוּא,
Hu!   תַּקִּיף הוּא,

Chorus: *Yiv'neh vei-to b'karov.
Bim'hera, bim'hera,
B'yameinu b'karov.
El B'neh! El B'neh!
B'neh veit'cha b'karov.

*יִבְנֶה בֵּיתוֹ בְּקָרוֹב,
בִּמְהֵרָה בִּמְהֵרָה,
בְּיָמֵינוּ בְּקָרוֹב.
אֵל בְּנֵה, אֵל בְּנֵה,
בְּנֵה בֵיתְךָ בְּקָרוֹב.

Holy, merciful, Almighty, powerful are You!
Chorus: *May You rebuild Your Temple.
Speedily, speedily, in our lifetime quickly.
O God, rebuild! O God, rebuild!
Rebuild Your Temple soon.

Who Knows One? אֶחָד מִי יוֹדֵעַ? Echad Mi Yo-de-a?

The "Number" Madrigal was added to the Haggadah in the fifteenth century. Though most number madrigals stop at twelve, the number thirteen is very important in Judaism. At thirteen, a boy and girl become Bar and Bat Mitzvah; thirteen are the creeds enumerated by Maimonides; thirteen are the attributes of God. Thirteen is the numerical value of the Hebrew letters in the word **Echad** (One), and refers to the unity of God, which is stressed throughout this selection.[38]

Directions: The leader(s) asks the questions and the participants answer.

Echad mi yo-de-a? Echad ani yo-de-a:
E-chad Eloheinu she-ba-shamayim
u-va-a-retz.

אֶחָד מִי יוֹדֵעַ? אֶחָד אֲנִי יוֹדֵעַ: אֶחָד
אֱלֹהֵינוּ שֶׁבַּשָּׁמַיִם וּבָאָרֶץ.

Who knows the answer to **one**?
I know the answer to One.
One is our God, in heaven and on earth.

Sh'na-yim mi yo-de-a? Sh'na-yim
ani yo-de-a: **Sh'nei lu-chot hab'rit,**
Echad Eloheinu She-ba-shamayim
u-va-a-retz.

שְׁנַיִם מִי יוֹדֵעַ? שְׁנַיִם אֲנִי יוֹדֵעַ:
שְׁנֵי לֻחוֹת הַבְּרִית, אֶחָד אֱלֹהֵינוּ
שֶׁבַּשָּׁמַיִם וּבָאָרֶץ

Who knows the answer to **two**?
I know the answer to two.
Two are Sinai's tablets.
But **One alone is our God**, in heaven and on earth.

Sh'lo-sha mi yo-de-a? Sh'lo-sha ani yo-de-a: **Sh'lo-sha avot**, Sh'nei lu-chot hab'rit, **Echad Eloheinu** she-ba-shamayim u-va-a-retz.

שְׁלֹשָׁה מִי יוֹדֵעַ? שְׁלֹשָׁה אֲנִי יוֹדֵעַ: שְׁלֹשָׁה אָבוֹת, שְׁנֵי לֻחוֹת הַבְּרִית, אֶחָד אֱלֹהֵינוּ שֶׁבַּשָּׁמַיִם וּבָאָרֶץ.

Who knows the answer to **three**?
I know the answer to three.
Three are the patriarchs; Two are Sinai's tablets.
But **One alone is our God**, in heaven and on earth.

Ar'ba mi yo-de-a? Ar'ba ani yo-de-a: **Ar'ba ima-hot**, Sh'lo-sha avot, Sh'nei lu-chot hab'rit, **Echad Eloheinu** she-ba-shamayim u-va-a-retz.

אַרְבַּע מִי יוֹדֵעַ? אַרְבַּע אֲנִי יוֹדֵעַ: אַרְבַּע אִמָּהוֹת, שְׁלֹשָׁה אָבוֹת, שְׁנֵי לֻחוֹת הַבְּרִית, אֶחָד אֱלֹהֵינוּ שֶׁבַּשָּׁמַיִם וּבָאָרֶץ.

I know the answer to four.
Four are the matriarchs;
Three are the patriarchs; Two are Sinai's tablets.
But **One alone is our God**, in heaven and on earth.

Cha-mi-sha mi yo-de-a? Cha-mi-sha ani yo-de-a: **Cha-mi-sha chum'shei Torah**, Ar'ba ima-hot, Sh'lo-sha avot, Sh'nei lu-chot hab'rit, **Echad Eloheinu** she-ba-shamayim u-va-a-retz.

חֲמִשָּׁה מִי יוֹדֵעַ? חֲמִשָּׁה אֲנִי יוֹדֵעַ: חֲמִשָּׁה חוּמְשֵׁי תוֹרָה, אַרְבַּע אִמָּהוֹת, שְׁלֹשָׁה אָבוֹת, שְׁנֵי לֻחוֹת הַבְּרִית, אֶחָד אֱלֹהֵינוּ שֶׁבַּשָּׁמַיִם וּבָאָרֶץ.

Who knows the answer to **five**?
I know the answer to five.
Five are the Books of Moses; Four are the matriarchs;
Three are the patriarchs; Two are Sinai's tablets.
But **One alone is our God**, in heaven and on earth.

Shi-sha mi yo-de-a? Shi-sha ani yo-de-a: **Shi-sha sid'rei Mish'na**; Cha-mi-sha chum'shei Torah, Ar'ba ima-hot, Sh'lo-sha avot, Sh'nei lu-chot hab'rit, **Echad Eloheinu** she-ba-shamayim u-va-a-retz.

שִׁשָּׁה מִי יוֹדֵעַ? שִׁשָּׁה אֲנִי יוֹדֵעַ: שִׁשָּׁה סִדְרֵי מִשְׁנָה, חֲמִשָּׁה חוּמְשֵׁי תוֹרָה, אַרְבַּע אִמָּהוֹת, שְׁלֹשָׁה אָבוֹת, שְׁנֵי לֻחוֹת הַבְּרִית, אֶחָד אֱלֹהֵינוּ שֶׁבַּשָּׁמַיִם וּבָאָרֶץ.

Who knows the answer to **six**?
I know the answer to six.
Six are the volumes of Mishnah;
Five are the Books of Moses; Four are the Matriarchs;
Three are the patriarchs; Two are Sinai's tablets.
But **One alone is our God**, in heaven and on earth.

Shiv'a mi yo-de-a? Shiv'a ani yo-de-a: **Shiv'a y'mei Sha-ba-ta**, Shi-sha sid'rei Mish'na, Cha-mi-sha chum'shei Torah, Ar'ba ima-hot, Sh'lo-sha avot, Sh'nei lu-chot hab'rit, **Echad Eloheinu** she-ba-shamayim u-va-a-retz.

שִׁבְעָה מִי יוֹדֵעַ? שִׁבְעָה אֲנִי יוֹדֵעַ: שִׁבְעָה יְמֵי שַׁבַּתָּא, שִׁשָּׁה סִדְרֵי מִשְׁנָה, חֲמִשָּׁה חוּמְשֵׁי תוֹרָה, אַרְבַּע אִמָּהוֹת, שְׁלֹשָׁה אָבוֹת, שְׁנֵי לֻחוֹת הַבְּרִית, אֶחָד אֱלֹהֵינוּ שֶׁבַּשָּׁמַיִם וּבָאָרֶץ.

Who knows the answer to **seven**?
I know the answer to seven.
Seven are the days of the week; Six are the volumes of Mishnah;
Five are the Books of Moses; Four are the matriarchs;
Three are the patriarchs; Two are Sinai's tablets.
But **One alone is our God**, in heaven and on earth.

Sh'mo-na mi yo-de-a? Sh'mo-na ani yo-de-a: **Sh'-mo-na y'mei milah**, Shiv'a y'mei Sha-ba-ta, Shi-sha sid'rei Mish'na, Cha-mi-sha chum'shei Torah, Ar'ba ima-hot, Sh'lo-sha avot, Sh'nei lu-chot hab'rit, **Echad Eloheinu** she-ba-shamayim u-va-a-retz.

שְׁמוֹנָה מִי יוֹדֵעַ? שְׁמוֹנָה אֲנִי יוֹדֵעַ: שְׁמוֹנָה יְמֵי מִילָה, שִׁבְעָה יְמֵי שַׁבַּתָּא, שִׁשָּׁה סִדְרֵי מִשְׁנָה, חֲמִשָּׁה חוּמְשֵׁי תוֹרָה, אַרְבַּע אִמָּהוֹת, שְׁלֹשָׁה אָבוֹת, שְׁנֵי לֻחוֹת הַבְּרִית, אֶחָד אֱלֹהֵינוּ שֶׁבַּשָּׁמַיִם וּבָאָרֶץ.

Who knows the answer to **eight**?
I know the answer to eight.
Eight are the days to the Covenant;
Seven are the days of the week; Six are the volumes of Mishnah;
Five are the Books of Moses; Four are the matriarchs;
Three are the patriarchs; Two are Sinai's tablets.
But **One alone is our God**, in heaven and on earth.

Tish'a mi yo-de-a? Tish'a ani yo-de-a: **Tish'a yar'chei le-da**, Sh'mo-na y'mei milah, Shiv'a y'mei Sha-ba-ta, Shi-sha sid'rei Mish'na, Cha-mi-sha chum'shei Torah, Ar'ba ima-hot, Sh'lo-sha avot, Sh'nei lu-chot hab'rit, **Echad Eloheinu** she-ba-shamayim u-va-a-retz.

תִּשְׁעָה מִי יוֹדֵעַ? תִּשְׁעָה אֲנִי יוֹדֵעַ: תִּשְׁעָה יַרְחֵי לֵדָה, שְׁמוֹנָה יְמֵי מִילָה, שִׁבְעָה יְמֵי שַׁבַּתָּא, שִׁשָּׁה סִדְרֵי מִשְׁנָה, חֲמִשָּׁה חוּמְשֵׁי תוֹרָה, אַרְבַּע אִמָּהוֹת, שְׁלֹשָׁה אָבוֹת, שְׁנֵי לֻחוֹת הַבְּרִית, אֶחָד אֱלֹהֵינוּ שֶׁבַּשָּׁמַיִם וּבָאָרֶץ.

Who knows the answer to nine?
I know the answer to nine.
Nine are the months to childbirth; Eight are the days to the covenant;
Seven are the days of the week; Six are the volumes of Mishnah;
Five are the Books of Moses; Four are the matriarchs;
Three are the patriarchs; Two are Sinai's tablets.
But **One alone is our God**, in heaven and on earth.

Nine
תִּשְׁעָה

A-sara mi yo-de-a? A-sara ani yo-de-a: **A-sara dib'ra-ya**, Tish'a yar'chei le-da, Sh'mo-na y'mei milah, Shiv'a y'mei Sha-ba-ta, Shi-sha sid'rei Mish-na, Cha-mi-sha chum'shei Torah, Ar'ba ima-hot, Sh'lo-sha avot, Sh'nei lu-chot hab'rit, **Echad Eloheinu** she-ba-shamayim u-va-a-retz.

עֲשָׂרָה מִי יוֹדֵעַ? עֲשָׂרָה אֲנִי יוֹדֵעַ: **עֲשָׂרָה דִבְּרַיָּא**, תִּשְׁעָה יַרְחֵי לֵדָה, שְׁמוֹנָה יְמֵי מִילָה, שִׁבְעָה יְמֵי שַׁבַּתָּא, שִׁשָּׁה סִדְרֵי מִשְׁנָה, חֲמִשָּׁה חוּמְשֵׁי תוֹרָה, אַרְבַּע אִמָּהוֹת, שְׁלֹשָׁה אָבוֹת, שְׁנֵי לֻחוֹת הַבְּרִית, **אֶחָד אֱלֹהֵינוּ** שֶׁבַּשָּׁמַיִם וּבָאָרֶץ.

Who knows the answer to **ten**?
I know the answer to ten.
Ten are the divine commandments;
Nine are the months to childbirth; Eight are the days to the covenant;
Seven are the days of the week; Six are the volumes of Mishnah;
Five are the Books of Moses; Four are the matriarchs;
Three are the patriarchs; Two are Sinai's tablets.
But **One alone is our God**, in heaven and on earth.

Ten
עֲשָׂרָה

Achad asar mi yo-de-a? A-chad asar ani yo-de-a: **Achad asar koch'va-ya**, A-sara dib'ra-ya, Tish'a yar'chei le-da, Sh'mo-na y'mei milah, Shiv'a y'mei Sha-ba-ta, Shi-sha sid'rei Mish-na, Cha-mi-sha chum'shei Torah, Ar'ba ima-hot, Sh'lo-sha avot, Sh'nei lu-chot hab'rit, **Echad Eloheinu** she-ba-shamayim u-va-a-retz.

אַחַד עָשָׂר מִי יוֹדֵעַ? אַחַד עָשָׂר אֲנִי יוֹדֵעַ: **אַחַד עָשָׂר כּוֹכְבַיָּא**, עֲשָׂרָה דִבְּרַיָּא, תִּשְׁעָה יַרְחֵי לֵדָה, שְׁמוֹנָה יְמֵי מִילָה, שִׁבְעָה יְמֵי שַׁבַּתָּא, שִׁשָּׁה סִדְרֵי מִשְׁנָה, חֲמִשָּׁה חוּמְשֵׁי תוֹרָה, אַרְבַּע אִמָּהוֹת, שְׁלֹשָׁה אָבוֹת, שְׁנֵי לֻחוֹת הַבְּרִית, **אֶחָד אֱלֹהֵינוּ** שֶׁבַּשָּׁמַיִם וּבָאָרֶץ.

Who knows the answer to **eleven**?
I know the answer to eleven.
Eleven are the stars in Joseph's dream;
Ten are the divine commandments;
Nine are the months to childbirth; Eight are the days to the covenant;
Seven are the days of the week; Six are the volumes of Mishnah;
Five are the Books of Moses; Four are the matriarchs;
Three are the patriarchs; Two are Sinai's tablets.
But **One alone is our God**, in heaven and on earth.

Sh'neim asar mi yo-de-a? Sh'neim asar ani yo-de-a. **Sh'neim asar shiv'ta-ya**, Achad asar koch'va-ya, A-sara dib'ra-ya, Tish'a yar'chei le-da, Sh'mo-na y'mei milah, Shiv'a y'mei Sha-ba-ta, Shi-sha sid'rei Mish'na, Cha-misha chum'shei Torah, Ar'ba ima-hot, Sh'lo-sha avot, Sh'nei lu-chot hab'rit, **Echad Eloheinu** she-ba-shamayim u-va-a-retz.

שְׁנֵים עָשָׂר מִי יוֹדֵעַ? שְׁנֵים עָשָׂר אֲנִי יוֹדֵעַ: שְׁנֵים עָשָׂר שִׁבְטַיָּא, אַחַד עָשָׂר כּוֹכְבַיָּא, עֲשָׂרָה דִבְּרַיָּא, תִּשְׁעָה יַרְחֵי לֵדָה, שְׁמוֹנָה יְמֵי מִילָה, שִׁבְעָה יְמֵי שַׁבַּתָּא, שִׁשָּׁה סִדְרֵי מִשְׁנָה, חֲמִשָּׁה חוּמְשֵׁי תוֹרָה, אַרְבַּע אִמָּהוֹת, שְׁלֹשָׁה אָבוֹת, שְׁנֵי לֻחוֹת הַבְּרִית, אֶחָד אֱלֹהֵינוּ שֶׁבַּשָּׁמַיִם וּבָאָרֶץ.

Who knows the answer to **twelve**?
I know the answer to twelve.
Twelve are the tribes of Israel;
Eleven are the stars in Joseph's dream; Ten are the divine commandments;
Nine are the months to childbirth; Eight are the days to the covenant;
Seven are the days of the week; Six are the volumes of Mishnah;
Five are the Books of Moses; Four are the matriarchs;
Three are the patriarchs; Two are Sinai's tablets.
But **One alone is our God**, in heaven and on earth.

Sh'lo-sha asar mi yo-de-a? Sh'lo-sha asar ani yo-dei-a. **Sh'lo-sha asar mi-da-ya,** Sh'neim asar shiv'ta-ya, Achad asar koch'va-ya, A-sara dib'ra-ya, Tish'a yar'chei le-da, Sh'mo-na y'mei milah, Shiv'a y'mei Sha-ba-ta, Shi-sha sid'rei Mish'na, Cha-misha chum'shei Torah, Ar'ba ima-hot, Sh'lo-sha avot, Sh'nei lu-chot hab'rit, **Echad Eloheinu** she-ba-shamayim u-va-a-retz.

שְׁלֹשָׁה עָשָׂר מִי יוֹדֵעַ? שְׁלֹשָׁה עָשָׂר אֲנִי יוֹדֵעַ: שְׁלֹשָׁה עָשָׂר מִדַּיָּא, שְׁנֵים עָשָׂר שִׁבְטַיָּא, אַחַד עָשָׂר כּוֹכְבַיָּא, עֲשָׂרָה דִבְּרַיָּא, תִּשְׁעָה יַרְחֵי לֵדָה, שְׁמוֹנָה יְמֵי מִילָה, שִׁבְעָה יְמֵי שַׁבַּתָּא, שִׁשָּׁה סִדְרֵי מִשְׁנָה, חֲמִשָּׁה חוּמְשֵׁי תוֹרָה, אַרְבַּע אִמָּהוֹת, שְׁלֹשָׁה אָבוֹת, שְׁנֵי לֻחוֹת הַבְּרִית, אֶחָד אֱלֹהֵינוּ שֶׁבַּשָּׁמַיִם וּבָאָרֶץ.

Who knows the answer to thirteen?

I know the answer to thirteen.

Thirteen are the attributes of God; *(Ex. 34: 6,7)*
Twelve are the tribes of Israel;
Eleven are the stars in Joseph's dream;
Ten are the divine commandments;
Nine are the months to childbirth; Eight are the days to the covenant;
Seven are the days of the week; Six are the volumes of Mishnah;
Five are the Books of Moses; Four are the matriarchs;
Three are the patriarchs; Two are Sinai's tablets.
But **One alone is our God**, in heaven and on earth.

One Little Goat   חַד גַּדְיָא   Chad Gadya

This medieval Aramaic song became a part of the Haggadah when it was included in the Prague edition of 1590. The popular song concludes the Seder on a happy note. But *Chad Gadya* is more than a simple jingle about a little goat purchased by a father for two coins. The central point is that retribution awaits every evil deed until the Redemption, when all evil is finally banished from the world and God's justice reigns supreme.

Viewed as an allegory of Jewish history, God (the Parent) redeemed Israel (the goat) through Moses and Aaron (the two *zuzim*), who succumbs to Assyria (the cat). Assyria is conquered by Babylonia (the dog), in turn struck down by Persia (the stick), which is devoured by Greece (the fire), extinguished by Rome (the water), defeated by the Saracens (the ox), beaten by the Crusaders (the slaughterer), conquered by the Turks (the angel of death), who is then killed by God.

Directions: Ask each volunteer to make a sound for his/her role in the song and to repeat his/her sound each time the role is mentioned.

Chad gad'ya, chad gad'ya,
(Chorus)*D'zabin aba bit'rei zu-zei,
Chad gad'ya, chad gad'ya.

חַד גַּדְיָא, חַד גַּדְיָא,
*דְּזַבִּין אַבָּא בִּתְרֵי זוּזֵי,
חַד גַּדְיָא, חַד גַּדְיָא.

One little goat! One little goat!
(Chorus)*My father bought for two zuzim.
One little goat! One little goat!

V'ata shun'ra v'ach'la l'gad'ya,
(Chorus)*D'zabin aba bit'rei zu-zei, Chad gad'ya, chad gad'ya.

וְאָתָא שׁוּנְרָא, וְאָכְלָה לְגַדְיָא,
*דְּזַבִּין אַבָּא בִּתְרֵי זוּזֵי,
חַד גַּדְיָא, חַד גַּדְיָא.

Then came a **cat** and ate the goat
(Chorus)*My father bought for two zuzim.
One little goat! One little goat!

V'ata **chal'ba** v'nashach l'shun'ra, d'ach'la l'gad'ya,
**(Chorus)*

וְאָתָא כַלְבָּא, וְנָשַׁךְ לְשׁוּנְרָא, דְּאָכְלָה לְגַדְיָא,*

Then came a **dog** that bit the cat that ate the goat **(Chorus)*

V'ata **chut'ra** v'hika l'chalba, d'nashach l'shunra, d'ach'la l'gad'ya. **(Chorus)*

וְאָתָא חוּטְרָא, וְהִכָּה לְכַלְבָּא, דְּנָשַׁךְ לְשׁוּנְרָא, דְּאָכְלָה לְגַדְיָא,*

Then came a **stick** and beat the dog that
bit the cat that ate the goat **(Chorus)*

V'ata **nura** v'saraf l'chut'ra,
d'hika l'chal'ba, d'nashach l'shun'ra,
d'ach'la l'gad'ya, **(Chorus)*

וְאָתָא נוּרָא, וְשָׂרַף לְחוּטְרָא,
דְּהִכָּה לְכַלְבָּא, דְּנָשַׁךְ לְשׁוּנְרָא,
דְּאָכְלָה לְגַדְיָא,*

Then came a fire and burned the stick that beat
the dog that bit the cat that ate the goat **(Chorus)*

V'ata **ma-ya** v'chava l'nura,
d'saraf l'chut'ra, d'hika l'chal'ba,
d'nashach l'shun'ra, d'ach'la
l'gad'ya, **(Chorus)*

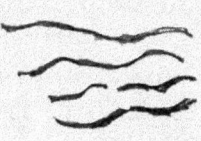

וְאָתָא מַיָּא, וְכָבָה לְנוּרָא, דְּשָׂרַף
לְחוּטְרָא, דְּהִכָּה לְכַלְבָּא,
דְּנָשַׁךְ לְשׁוּנְרָא, דְּאָכְלָה לְגַדְיָא,*

Then came water and quenched the fire that burned the stick that beat the dog that bit
the cat that ate the goat **(Chorus)*

V'ata **tora** v'shata l'ma-ya, d'chava l'nura, d'saraf l'chut'ra, d'hika l'chal'ba, d'nashach l'shun'ra, d'ach'la l'gad'ya, *(Chorus)*

וְאָתָא תוֹרָא, וְשָׁתָא לְמַיָּא, דְּכָבָה לְנוּרָא, דְּשָׂרַף לְחוּטְרָא, דְּהִכָּה לְכַלְבָּא, דְּנָשַׁךְ לְשׁוּנְרָא, דְּאָכְלָה לְגַדְיָא,*

Then came an **ox** and drank the water that quenched the fire that burned the stick that beat the dog that bit the cat that ate the goat *(Chorus)*

V'ata **hashochet** v'shachat l'tora, d'shata l'ma-ya, d'chava l'nura, d'saraf l'chut'ra, d'hika l'chal'ba, d'nashach l'shun'ra, d'ach'la l'gad'ya, *(Chorus)*

וְאָתָא הַשּׁוֹחֵט, וְשָׁחַט לְתוֹרָא, דְּשָׁתָא לְמַיָּא, דְּכָבָה לְנוּרָא, דְּשָׂרַף לְחוּטְרָא, דְּהִכָּה לְכַלְבָּא, דְּנָשַׁךְ לְשׁוּנְרָא, דְּאָכְלָה לְגַדְיָא,*

Then came a **slaughterer** and killed the ox that drank the water that quenched the fire that burned the stick that beat the dog that bit the cat that ate the goat *Chorus)*

V'ata **mal'ach ha-mavet**, v'shachat l'shochet, d'shachat l'tora, d'shata l'ma-ya, d'chava l'nura, d'saraf l'chut'ra, d'hika l'chal'ba, d'nashach l'shun'ra, d'ach'la l'gad'ya, *(Chorus)*

וְאָתָא מַלְאַךְ הַמָּוֶת, וְשָׁחַט לְשׁוֹחֵט, דְּשָׁחַט לְתוֹרָא, דְּשָׁתָא לְמַיָּא, דְּכָבָה לְנוּרָא, דְּשָׂרַף לְחוּטְרָא, דְּהִכָּה לְכַלְבָּא, דְּנָשַׁךְ לְשׁוּנְרָא, דְּאָכְלָה לְגַדְיָא,*

Then came the **angel of death** and slew the slaughterer who killed the ox that drank the water that quenched the fire that burned the stick that beat the dog that bit the cat that ate the goat *(Chorus)*

V'ata **Ha-Kadosh Baruch Hu**, v'shachat l'mal'ach ha-mavet d'shachat l'shochet, d'shachat l'tora, d'shata l'ma-ya, d'chava l'nura, d'saraf l'chut'ra, d'hika l'chal'ba, d'nashach l'shunra, d'ach'la l'gadya, ***D'zabin aba bit'rei zu-zei, Chad gad'ya, chad gad'ya.**

וְאָתָא הַקָּדוֹשׁ בָּרוּךְ הוּא, וְשָׁחַט לְמַלְאַךְ הַמָּוֶת, דְּשָׁחַט לְשׁוֹחֵט, דְּשָׁחַט לְתוֹרָא, דְּשָׁתָא לְמַיָּא, דְּכָבָה לְנוּרָא, דְּשָׂרַף לְחוּטְרָא, דְּהִכָּה לְכַלְבָּא, דְּנָשַׁךְ לְשׁוּנְרָא, דְּאָכְלָה לְגַדְיָא, *דְּזַבִּין אַבָּא בִּתְרֵי זוּזֵי, חַד גַּדְיָא, חַד גַּדְיָא.

Then came the **Holy One, praised are You**, and smote the angel of death who slew the slaughterer who killed the ox that drank the water that quenched the fire that burned the stick that beat the dog that bit the cat that ate the goat

*My father bought for two zuzim. One little goat! One little goat!

In these times when the rights of so many are so much debated and discussed, it occurs to me that some human rights, universal in scope, are being overlooked. Lest we forget, I now claim those rights for you and myself—and any others who have the will.

I have the right to:

1. Love the people who are so difficult to love as to seem unworthy.
2. Work for the common good of humankind even though at times it seems I toil alone.
3. Maintain standards of absolute love, purity, honesty, and unselfishness as guidelines for my daily living.
4. Give encouragement and support as often as possible to as many as possible.
5. Assume responsibility for the consequences of all my conscious acts.
6. Befriend the friendless.
7. Have my destiny defined on the merits of my behavior.
8. Err, to fail, to begin anew, to learn, to atone, to aspire . . .
9. A fair mixture of life's blessings and ills in the pursuit of liberty and peace.
10. Live and die with a self-defined dignity.

For you, your friends, myself, my friends and all other human beings I declare and defend such rights.
E. Ramonia Longs

Closing Prayer

Passover marks the birthday of the Jewish people. Just as a child is freed from the constraints and limitations of the womb at birth, the Jewish people were freed from the physical limitations of Egyptian slavery and the spiritual constraints of Egyptian idolatry and culture. How can we best honor and celebrate the birthday of our people?[39]

God has given each of us a purpose in life–to commit and encourage acts of goodness, to use our time, energy, and knowledge to tear through the layers of the "container" in which we live in order to reveal God's light within. Despite the lack of a satisfactory answer to the question of evil, one can–and must–carry on a meaningful life, promote justice and kindness, and, indeed, help create a better world, one in which there is no nourishment for evil, where there is no room in one's heart for any inhumanity whatsoever.[40]

America - words by Samuel F. Smith

My country 'tis of thee,
Sweet land of liberty,
Of thee I sing;
Land where [my people strive],
Land of [my parent's pride],
From every mountainside
Let freedom ring.

Hatikva הַתִּקְוָה

Kol od ba-levav p'nimah
Nefesh y'hudi homi-yah
U-l'fa-atei miz'rach kadimah
Ayin l'tzi-on tzofi-yah
Od lo av'da tik'va-tenu
Hatik'va sh'not al'pa-yim
Lih'yot am chaf'shi b'ar'tzenu
Eretz tzi-on vi-Ru-sha-la-yim.

כָּל עוֹד בַּלֵּבָב פְּנִימָה
נֶפֶשׁ יְהוּדִי הוֹמִיָּה,
וּלְפַאֲתֵי מִזְרָח קָדִימָה
עַיִן לְצִיּוֹן צוֹפִיָּה.
עוֹד לֹא אָבְדָה תִּקְוָתֵנוּ,
הַתִּקְוָה שְׁנוֹת אַלְפַּיִם,
לִהְיוֹת עַם חָפְשִׁי בְּאַרְצֵנוּ,
בְּאֶרֶץ צִיּוֹן וִירוּשָׁלָיִם.

As long as, in our innermost heart,
A Jewish soul stirs,
And as long as, to the furthermost east,
Our eyes look to Zion,
Then our two thousand year hope
To be a free nation in our land, Zion,
Is not lost.

Appendix

Excerpted from an article by George F. Will appearing in the Washington Post in March 1983.

Americans have a habit of looking on the bright side of life. But occasionally, it is salutary to look at the dark side. We can do this in Washington, D.C., at the Holocaust Museum.

But some persons will ask: What has the Holocaust to do with this nation? That is a fair question. The answer is that no other nation has broader, graver responsibilities in the world, so no other nation more needs citizens trained to look life in the face.

Leave aside the scandal of this nation and its allies–the fact that they did not act on the knowledge that the Holocaust was occurring. They refused, for example, to bomb the rail lines and crematoria at Auschwitz when 10,000 were dying there daily. Never mind. The museum should be an institution of understanding, not accusation.

The theme of the Holocaust memorial in Jerusalem is **Remember!** But remembrance without understanding is betrayal. It occurs when people try to democratize the Holocaust,

We falsify and trivialize the Holocaust when we bend it to our convenience, making it a symbol of general beastliness, or whatever. It was not a symbol; it was a fact. The flight into such generalities is a flinching from this fact: The Holocaust was directed murderously against particular victims: Jews. Their tragedy cannot be appropriated by others as a useful metaphor.

But a general good for the nation can flow from an unblinking understanding of it.

The two shattering events of modern politics were the First World War and The Holocaust. The war shattered governments and empires, and patterns of civility, clearing the ground for primitivism. The Holocaust–the eruption of primitivism in the heart of our civilization–overturned the idea that there are limits on evil.

What is life like when lived beyond a sense of limits? You could tell from the smoke the sort of persons consumed in the crematoria. Newcomers to Auschwitz, who still had some fat on their bones, made black smoke. Persons who had been there for a while made white smoke. That is an emblematic fact of 20th century politics.

The Holocaust was the bureaucratization, almost the domestication, of the most volatile passion, hatred. The memory of the Holocaust is the black sun into which we cannot bear to stare.

And the Holocaust Museum is a reminder that nothing in nature is more remarkable, or dangerous, than the recuperative power of innocence in a liberal society.

Appendix: Quantities to Be Consumed at the Seder Table:

Wine:
    3.38 fluid ounces per cup
    4.42 fluid ounces for the first cup if the Seder falls on a Friday night

Matzah:
Scholars differ concerning the exact volume that an "olive" size portion constitutes. The following amounts reflect the range of fluctuation that exists:

    7" × 6¼", 26 grams,
    0.845 fluid ounces,
    1 fluid ounce,
    a small portion

Maror:
    Horseradish: 0.7 fluid ounce, 1.1 fluid ounces, 19 grams, a small portion
    Romaine stalks: 3" × 5", 1.1 fluid ounces, 19 grams, a small portion
    Romaine lettuce leaves: 8" × 10", 1.1 fluid ounces, 19 grams, a small portion

Sources

I have attempted to list below the sources used in this Haggadah. Unless otherwise noted, the selections listed below have been adapted or modified by me. I am also responsible for all unattributed material. I would like to apologize to any author, whether living or dead, who should have been credited and was not.

[1] Rabbi Shlomo Riskin, ***The Passover Haggadah*** (New York: Ktav Publishing House, Inc., 1983), p. 36.

[2] Rabbi Yaakov Culi, ***The Passover Haggadah MeAm Lo'ez***, trans. Rabbi Aryeh Kaplan (New York and Jerusalem: Maznaim Publishing Corp., 1978), p. 94.

[3] Culi, 6.

[4] ***The Haggadah***, trans. Rabbi Joseph Elias (New York: Mesorah Publications, Ltd., 1977), p. li.

[5] Rabbi Morris Silverman (ed.), ***The Passover Haggadah*** 3rd ed. rev.; (Bridgeport: The Prayer Book Press, 1975), p. 2.

[6] Riskin, 38.

[7] Ibid., 47.

[8] Rabbi Menachem M. Kasher (ed.), ***Israel Passover Haggadah*** (New York: Shengold Publishers, Inc., 1983), p. 51.

[9] Rabbi Avrohom Davis, ***The Metsudah Linear Haggadah*** (Hoboken: Ktav Publishing House, Inc., 1993), p. x.

[10] Rabbi Abraham J. Twerski, M.D., ***From Bondage to Freedom*** (New York: Shaar Press, 1995), p. 78.

[11] Aviva Cantor, ***An Egalitarian Hagada*** (New York: Beruriah Books, 2000), p. 11.

[12] Culi, 41.

[13] Riskin, 79.

[14] Culi, 50.

[15] Ibid.

[16] Cantor, 14.

[17] Ibid.

[18] Jane Sprague Zones (ed.), ***San Diego Women's Haggadah*** 2nd ed. (San Diego: Woman's Institute for Continuing Jewish Education, 1986), p. 35.

[19] Ibid.

[20] Riskin, 84.

[21] Cantor, 12.

[22] Sprague Zones, 35.

[23] Cantor, 12.
[24] Ibid.
[25] Riskin, 86.
[26] Rabbi Dr. Marcus Lehmann, *Passover Hagadah* (London: J. Lehman, 1969), p. 134.
[27] Ibid., 144.
[28] Cantor, 12.
[29] Ibid, 13.
[30] Ibid.
[31] Ibid.
[32] Culi, 91.
[33] Kaplan, Mordecai, Kohn, Eugene, and Eisenstein, Ira (eds.), *The New Haggadah* 2nd ed. rev. (New York: Behrman House Inc., 1978), pp. 65-66.
[34] Riskin, 27-28.
[35] Ibid., 107.
[36] Silverman, 46.
[37] Riskin, 134.
[38] Silverman, 72.
[39] Yehudis Cohen, **"On Birthdays and Freedom,"** *L'Chaim,* Issue 465 (Apr. 18/25, 1997), p. 1.
[40] Rabbi Menachem Mendel Schneerson, *Toward a Meaningful Life: The Wisdom of the Rebbe*, adapted by Rabbi Simon Jacobson, (New York: William Morrow & Co., Inc., 1995) p. 264.

Illustration Credits

I have attempted to list below the sources used in this Haggadah for the illustrations and the pages on which they appear in the Haggadah. Unless otherwise noted, the illustrations listed below have been adapted or modified by me. I am also responsible for all unattributed illustrations.

Charlotte Z. Gould–Haggadah cover; Baruch page 5; Seder Plate page 10; matzot pages iii, iv, v, 1, 4, 6, 8, 10, 11, 29, 51; Four Children pages 27–28; Ten Plagues page 43; stars page 75; Seder objects page 107.
Ira Steingroot, *Keeping Passover*, © 1995, Harper San Francisco: overlay order/meaning of symbols on Seder Plate according to the sixteenth-century Rabbi Isaac Luria, the Ari of Safed, page 10, by permission of Ira Steingroot.
Chayim Ehrenfeld–Hebrews leaving Egypt, page 44.
Kevin Powell–Moses parting the waters, page 57.
Irene Rodman Helitzer–Miriam's Cup, page 72 (photo by R. C. Richman).
Honey Meir-Levi–Elijah's Cup, page 72 (photo by R. C. Richman).
David Wolfe–Sabbath and Festival Candelabra, page 82 (photo by R. C. Richman).
A.R.E. Publishing, Inc.–Jerusalem scene, page 87.
Former Students of The Agnon School, Beachwood, Ohio, with gratitude to **Karen Lazar**, Former Director of Development and Barbara Weiss, former Art Teacher:
    Vitaly Neyman–Moses, page 7.
    Arthur Simonovskiy–wine decanter and glasses, page 12.
    Hallie Brooks–four cups of wine, page 12.
    Laura Joseph–wine goblet, pages 16, 58, 71, 86.
    Shira Polster–wine goblet, page 18.
    Lanna Justmann–Aramean scene, page 24; two women pages 31, 37, 39.
    Sharon Brzezinski–Egyptian slave scene, page 35; Moses, page 39; chariot scene, page 57.
    Justine Kunstler–Egptian slave scene-bottom of page 36.
    Todd Zeiger–baby Moses, page 38.
    Ariella Kirsch–Passover scenes and symbols, page 54.
    Andrew Waxman–Moses with the Ten Commandments, page 92.
    Alla Fabrikant–Passover table scene, page 105.

Copyrights Acknowledgments

The publisher has made every effort to trace the ownership of all copyrighted material and to secure permission from holders of such material. Any omissions or errors are deeply regretted, and the publisher, upon notification, will be pleased to make necessary corrections in future printings. The publisher wishes to thank the following authors, publishers, and publications for their kind permission to reprint the material indicated.

Beacon Press: From *Man's Search for Meaning* by Viktor E. Frankl. © 1959, 1963 by Viktor E. Frankl. Reprinted by permission of Beacon Press.

Behrman House Inc: *"We are commanded. . ."* from *The New Haggadah* © 1941, 1978 edited by Mordecai Kaplan, Eugene Kohn, and Ira Eisenstein. Reprinted by permission of Behrman House, Inc.

Aviva Cantor: *"Freedom from a master"* from *An Egalitarian Hagada*, Beruriah Books POB 1874 Cathedral Station, NY NY 10023-1874 © 2000. Used with permission.

Central Conference of American Rabbis: *"Order of the Service"* by Malcolm H. Stern; *"And God Knew..."* by Herbert Bronstein from *A Passover Haggadah* © 1974, 1975. Reprinted by permission of the Central Conference of American Rabbis.

Yehudis Cohen: *"Karpas and Spring."* Used with permission.

Gary M. Klein: *"Immigrants and Strangers."*

E. Ramonia Longs: *"What can I do to hasten that day"* and *"In these times."* Used with permission.

Craig Lynch: *"SEDER."* Used with permission.

William Morrow and Co.: *"God has given each of us a purpose in life"* from *Toward a Meaningful Life, The Wisdom of the Rebbe, Menachem Mendel Schneerson*, adapted by Simon Jacobson, © 1995 by Vaad Hanochos Hatmimim. Reprinted by permission.

News America Publishing, Inc.: *"Chosen people wear yoke not superiority complex"* by Sydney J. Harris. Reprinted by permission.

Pantheon Henry Holt 1989/1996 eds: From *An Interrupted Life: The Diaries of Etty Hillesum, 1941–1943*. © 1996 by Eva Hoffman. Reprinted by permission of Random House, Inc. and Henry Holt.

Judy Petsonk: *"Seder holds lesson for all of us,"* author of *Taking Judaism Personally: Creating a Meaningful Spiritual Life*. © 1996 by Judy Petsonk. The Free Press. Used with permission.

Rabbi Menachem Mendel Schneerson: *"The Fifth Child."* Used with permission.

Schocken Books: *"There are Stars"* From *Hannah Senesh: Her Life and Diary*. © 1972 reprinted by permission of Random House ©1971 reprinted by permission of Vallentine Mitchell & Co..

George F. Will: *"Holocaust Museum"* © 1983, The Washington Post Writers Group. Reprinted with permission.

Seder Menus and Recipes

PASSOVER SEDER MENU SUGGESTIONS

I have two Seders at my house each year. In the past, I varied the menu for each Seder night. Presently, I use the same menu for both nights to simplify the process and cut down on preparation time.

   Recipes for items that have an asterisk in front of them appear in the Recipe section of this book.

FIRST AND SECOND NIGHT

Shmurah Matzah
Kosher for Passover Wine and/or Grape Juice

Seder Plate and Table: Beitzah (Roasted Egg), Z'ro-a (Roasted Shankbone), Maror (Bitter Herbs), Kar'pas (Green Vegetables), *Charoset (Chopped fruit, nuts, spices, and wine), Chazeret (Additional Maror), Orange, Salt Water, Matzah Plate and cover

Appetizers: Hard-Boiled Eggs, *Gefilte Fish with Horseradish, *Roasted Eggplant Spread, *Kishka, *Marinated Zucchini, Pitchers of Cold Water with Lemon or Orange Slices

Soup: *Chicken Soup with Knaidlach

Salad and Vegetables: Fresh Vegetable Salad with *French Dressing

Main Dish: *Roast Brisket, *Duck Sauce Chicken

Kugels: *Sweet Potato Blueberry Kugel, *Spinach Mushroom Kugel

Fruit: Fresh, cut up Fruit

Dessert: *Lemon Chiffon Cake, *Chocolate Torte, *Almond Clusters, *Mandelbread, Hot Tea

Example of a Passover Shopping List

Consult your rabbi for items that do not require Kosher for Passover label.

Passover Shopping List Year (Quantities for Two Seders)

At Least Two-Three Weeks before Passover

1 small cream rose or cream red concord medium sweet wine for cooking
2 large bottles grape juice
4 bottles blush or zinfandel wine
4 bottles lightly sweet red wine
3 bottles Merlot
1 box parchment paper
Ziplock bags, all sizes
1 16 oz. pkg. potato starch
2 boxes cake meal
2 boxes matzah meal
1 box Shmurah matzah 2 boxes matzah
2 boxes farfel
Passover baking powder
1 qt. safflower oil (don't need if get grape seed oil)
50 oz. grape seed oil
1 lb. soft pareve margarine (as healthy as possible)
10 lbs. sugar
1 lb. brown sugar
1 lb. confectionery sugar, if available
cocoa
2 boxes matzah ball only mix
6 cubes chicken soup flavor (meat)
1 large container chicken flavor, (meat) instant powder soup mix
1 box (2 packets) onion soup
1¼ lbs. sliced almonds
1 lb walnuts for charoset/chocolate torte
1 bar (14 oz) semisweet chocolate
1 bag chocolate chips
1 small jar white vinegar
1 small jar wine vinegar
1 small jar ketchup
2 boxes Shake N Bake
1 jar duck sauce, Cantonese sweet & sour
orange juice for chicken
paprika/turmeric
dill weed
poultry seasoning
Italian seasoning
parsley
onion powder
garlic powder
salt/pepper
coarse kosher salt
nutmeg
cinnamon
ginger
cloves
vanilla
imitation butter flavor
coffee, herbal teas
1-25 oz. jar tomato sauce
2-8 oz. cans tomato sauce for gefilte fish
1 12 oz. can tomato paste for eggplant
1 small can applesauce
3 boxes frozen chopped spinach
3-12 oz. pkgs. frozen blueberries for sweet potato kugel
4-5 rolls frozen gefilte fish
2 lbs./32 oz. fresh portobello mushrooms for spinach kugel/ brisket, don't buy until ready to use
9-10 dozen eggs
1 small jar horseradish

fresh garlic cloves
1 sweet potato for chicken soup
3½–4 lbs. sweet potatoes, ¾–1 lb. each. Buy when ready to make kugel (scrape skin—dark orange/ purple)
6 lbs. mild onions
4 lbs. carrots, not too large
10 Golden Delicious apples for chocolate cake, charoset
5 medium eggplants, 1 lb. size, don't buy until ready to use
5 large ripe firm tomatoes for eggplant spread
6 lemons
4 oranges for drinking water
4 ripe bananas, pancakes/cake
2 medium parsnips
4½-6 lbs. lean flank steak roast, big piece, or veal brisket
1 shank bone
3-4 pkgs. (3 lbs. each) frozen chicken split breasts w/bones
3 pullets for soup

Disposable/Plastic/Paper Goods
8- 9"×12"×2½" disposable aluminum pans for spinach and sweet potato kugels

On Table Before Seder:
2 each plastic tablecloths for each night
1 each wine glass
1 each dessert plate
1 each napkin and spoon

Mealtime Appetizers:
1 each 9" plate, napkin, water glass, fork

Soup and Main Meal:
1 each soup bowl, soup spoon, 10½" dinner plate, fork, knife

Dessert:
1 each dessert plate, small fruit compote dish, cup for tea, forks, and spoons

Approximately two days before Seder
6–8 zucchini
1 head romaine
1 small bunch parsley
horseradish root
salad greens

PASSOVER SEDER RECIPES

PASSOVER CHAROSET (PAREVE)

6 Golden Delicious apples, peeled and coarsely chopped
1 cup walnuts, chopped
1 teaspoon cinnamon or more
Ginger to taste
1 teaspoon lemon rind
1 cup sweet red wine, approximately

Put nuts in food processor; process using on-off switch until desired consistency is reached. Process the apples until coarsely chopped. Combine all ingredients, adding wine in small quantities as you mix. Reserve the bulk of wine and add just before the Seder begins. This gives the charoset a brighter color and prevents bleeding. Refrigerate and stir occasionally.

GEFILTE FISH (PAREVE)   *Yehudis Cohen*

Preheat oven to 375°F.

2 frozen raw gefilte fish rolls
—approximately 22 oz. each
⅔ cup tomato sauce

Remove all paper from frozen fish rolls. Place in a 9"×13" baking pan lined with aluminum foil. Spoon approximately ⅓ cup of tomato sauce over each roll. Cover pan tightly with aluminum foil. Bake in the oven for approximately 1 hour and 45 minutes. If the pan has a lot of liquid remaining, bake for another 10–15 minutes. If baking only one fish roll, use a smaller pan, set oven temperature at 350°F and bake for 1 hour and 30 minutes. The fish rolls expand in the baking process. Cool the fish rolls and refrigerate until ready to use. Then slice and place on a large platter or on individual plates. Serve with horseradish. This is a delicious easy alternative to making your own gefilte fish. Each roll serves approximately 8–10 people, depending on the thickness of the slices.

Variation: Partially defrost frozen roll of gefilte fish for 10 minutes. Cover a large cookie sheet with aluminum foil. Coat foil with a vegetable spray. Cut gefilte fish roll into ¾-inch slices and place on cookie sheet. Sprinkle Italian seasoning on each slice. Bake in 350°F preheated oven until lightly brown on top and bottom, approximately 20–25 minutes.

ROASTED EGGPLANT SPREAD (PAREVE) — *Judy Rosenberg*

Preheat oven to 400°F.

- 3 medium eggplants, peeled and cut into 1 inch cubes
- 1–1½ tablespoons kosher salt
- 6 tablespoons olive, canola, or grape seed oil*
- 8–10 garlic cloves, minced
- 5 large tomatoes, cut in chunks
- 12 oz. tomato paste
- 1–1½ tablespoons fresh lemon juice
- ½ teaspoon sugar
- ¼ teaspoon black pepper

Combine eggplant, salt, and oil. Spread mixture on large foil-lined baking sheet. Roast uncovered for 30 minutes. Reduce heat to 325°F. Combine rest of ingredients, spread on top of eggplant, and cover with foil. Return to oven and bake 60 minutes. Cool and combine well. Taste and adjust seasonings.

*At Passover, use Kosher for Passover oil.

PASSOVER KISHKA (PAREVE)

Preheat oven to 375°F.

- ⅓ cup melted Kosher for Passover margarine
- ¼ cup Kosher for Passover grape seed or safflower oil
- 2 cups onions, coarsely chopped
- 4 stalks celery, cut into 1-inch pieces
- 4 large carrots, coarsely chopped
- 1¼ teaspoon garlic powder
- ¼ cup chicken broth
- 2 teaspoons salt
- ¼ teaspoon pepper
- 2 eggs and 2 egg whites, beaten
- Dash of sugar
- 4 tablespoons dry parsley
- 2 cups matzah meal

Sauté onions in oil and margarine until tender, about 5–10 minutes. Do not brown the onions. Put matzah meal in a large bowl. Put all other ingredients including onions, oil, and melted margarine (except parsley) into food processor. Process until finely chopped. Add parsley and pour over matzah meal; mix well. If mixture is too dry, add a little more chicken soup. Cut four pieces of foil approximately 16 inches wide. Grease foil lightly with oil. Divide the mixture into four rolls on the foil sheets. Wrap the foil up loosely to allow for expansion and twist ends to seal. Place rolls on a cookie sheet and bake for 45 minutes if freezing and 60 minutes if not freezing. Remove foil, slice, and serve or freeze, defrost, and reheat in foil; slice and serve.

Marinated Zucchini (Pareve)

2 tablespoons oil
2 tablespoons sugar
¼ cup wine vinegar
4 tablespoons filtered water
1 teaspoon salt

⅛ teaspoon pepper
1 teaspoon dill weed
Snipped chives to taste
6 medium zucchini, washed and sliced

Combine all marinade ingredients; mix until sugar is dissolved. Pour over sliced zucchini. Put in tight-lidded container. Marinate for several hours to overnight in refrigerator, basting occasionally. This marinade can be used on cut red, yellow, and orange peppers, broccoli, and/or carrots. Will keep in the refrigerator for 3–4 days.

Chicken Soup with Knaidlach (Meat)

Chicken Soup

8–9 lbs. chicken (1 cut-up pullet with skin plus extra legs, thighs, necks, and backs)
Cloth mesh boil bags
6 large carrots, washed
4 large onions, unpeeled
2–3 large parsnips, washed
2–3 large turnips, washed
2 whole clusters garlic cloves with skin

2 bunches of fresh dill, rinsed and tied with string
1 tablespoon salt
¼ teaspoon black pepper
Chicken bouillon cubes
Pinch of ground ginger, optional
½ teaspoon lemon juice, optional
⅛ teaspoon tumeric, optional

Place chicken, chicken parts, and vegetables i n cloth mesh boil bags, knot each bag and place in large stock pot. Add fi ltered water to exceed chicken and vegetables by 2 inches. Bring to a boil over high heat; skim off foam that rises to surface. Reduce heat to low so liquid is barely simmering; add dill, cover, and continue cooking 3–5 hours. Turn off heat. Remove chicken and vegetable bags from liquid and place in colander over a container to catch liquid. Remove garlic clusters from vegetable bag and discard. Save chicken, carrots, and parsnips. Strain soup in a colander. Refrigerate soup, chicken, and vegetables. Remove congealed fat from soup. Place soup, chicken, carrots, and parsnips (in their cloth mesh boil bags) in stock pot, bring to boil and simmer for 2 more hours. Remove chicken and vegetables. Add salt and pepper. Add chicken bouillon cubes and a pinch of ginger to taste. May be refrigerated for 2 days or frozen for future use. If you add matzah meal dumplings when reheating soup, keep lid on without removing. This further increases size of dumplings.

KNAIDLACH MATZAH MEAL SOUP DUMPLINGS (PAREVE)

1 package matzo ball mix (There are many from which to choose.)
1 egg plus 2 egg whites
2 tablespoons canola oil
2 tablespoons pareve chicken broth
2½ quarts of boiling water or soup

Combine the eggs, oil, and chicken broth in a medium size mixing bowl; whisk together, but do not whip. Sprinkle the contents of one bag of matzo ball mix into the egg mixture. Stir with a fork, mixing as little as possible. Cover and chill in the refrigerator for 20 minutes. Bring water or broth to boil. Add 2 teaspoons of salt to water. (If using soup, do not add salt). Using wet hands, form balls the size of a walnut shell, handling and using as little pressure as possible. Add matzo balls to the boiling liquid. Cook in a covered pot with a simmer-low flame for 20 minutes. Do not lift lid during cooking. If using water, remove matzo balls with slotted spoon and add to soup. If cooking in soup, leave the matzo balls in the soup and keep warm until ready to serve. Matzo balls freeze well in soup. They can also be frozen without liquid in a single layer on a cookie sheet. When frozen, they can be transferred to a plastic ziplock bag.

FRENCH DRESSING (PAREVE)

Rhoda Shapiro

1 teaspoon salt
½–1 teaspoon sugar
¼ teaspoon paprika
¼ cup cider vinegar
¾ cup grapeseed oil
1 clove garlic, peeled and split.
Dash of black pepper

Combine all ingredients. Shake well with each use.

BRISKET (MEAT)

4½ pounds lean brisket, flank steak, or veal brisket
1 package onion soup
½ cup burgundy wine
½ cup Heinz ketchup™
¼ cup water
2 tablespoon brown sugar
¼ teaspoon ginger powder
½ teaspoon garlic powder
Pepper and paprika to taste
8–12 oz. fresh mushrooms, sliced before final heating

Remove as much fat from brisket as possible, rinse, and dry. Sear brisket on all surfaces in heated heavy Dutch oven or 12" fry pan. Put fat-side up in pan after searing. Sprinkle onion soup and seasonings on top. Combine wine, ketchup, and water, and pour over top. Seal top with heavy duty aluminum foil. Place heavy lid over foil to seal in moisture. Roast in oven at 325°F temperature for 2½–3 hours depending on cut of meat. Brisket takes longer to roast, while veal and flank steak take less time. Cool and refrigerate overnight. Skim fat from gravy. Roast can be sliced at this point or frozen whole to be sliced later. If frozen, defrost in refrigerator, then slice. Return sliced meat to gravy in an oven-proof serving dish. Top with fresh sliced mushrooms, spooning some gravy over the mushrooms. Cover and reheat in oven at 300°F for 30–45 minutes or until well-heated. Spoon some gravy over the meat and mushrooms before serving.

Passover Duck Sauce Chicken (Meat)

Preheat oven to 475°F.

5 chicken breasts, skinned and cut into serving pieces
1 large jar Passover sweet and sour mild duck sauce
½ cup orange juice or more
1 package Passover "Shake and Bake"
¼ teaspoon ground ginger

Place oven rack on bottom slot. Spray a nonstick baking pan with cooking spray or lightly grease with oil. Put Shake and Bake mixture with ground ginger into gallon size plastic bag and mix well. Drop two pieces of chicken into bag at a time and shake to coat. Arrange coated chicken in a single layer on prepared pan and bake approximately 10 minutes on each side until lightly brown. Reduce heat to 350°F. Brush chicken generously on each side with duck sauce. Pour orange juice over chicken. Bake 30 minutes uncovered. Brush frequently with sauce. Cover and continue baking and basting until tender. Add more orange juice if needed.

Sweet Potato Blueberry Kugel (Pareve)

Preheat oven to 350°F.

6 sweet potatoes (not yams), about 2½ to 3½ pounds
10 large carrots, about 1½ pounds
3 eggs and 8 egg whites
2 tablespoons potato starch
⅔ cup matzo cake flour (or 1 cup regular flour)
1 teaspoon Passover baking powder or regular baking powder
1 cup brown sugar, packed
½ cup oil
⅓ cup applesauce
2 teaspoons cinnamon
2 teaspoons vanilla
1 teaspoon nutmeg
½ teaspoon salt

Peel potatoes and carrots. Cut into one-inch chunks. Cover with water and lid. Boil until tender. Drain, cool and puree with eggs in food processor. Add rest of ingredients to potato mixture and mix well. Spray two 8"×10" disposable aluminum pans with nonstick spray. Put half of potato mixture in bottom of the two pans. Spread blueberry mixture over; cover with remaining potato mixture. Bake for approximately 1 hour and 20 minutes. Bake less if freezing. Knife in center should come out fairly clean. Let stand 30 minutes before serving.

Blueberry filling

2 (16 oz.) packages of frozen blueberries
½ cup sugar
1 cup water
1½–2 tablespoons potato starch (or 2 tablespoons arrowroot)
1½ tablespoons lemon juice
Pinch of salt

Put one package of berries in medium pot with water, sugar, potato starch, lemon juice, and salt. Cook and stir until thickens. Cool 15 minutes. Add second package of frozen berries and mix gently.

SPINACH MUSHROOM KUGEL (PAREVE)

Preheat oven to 375°F.

1 pound matzo farfel
4 cups water
2 (10 oz.) packages frozen spinach, thawed and drained
1 cup onion, coarsely grated
2 celery stalks, chopped
2 cloves garlic, crushed
1 tablespoon dry parsley
1 teaspoon dry dill weed
2 tablespoons fresh lemon juice
1 tablespoon salt
⅛–¼ teaspoon pepper
24 oz. mushrooms, sliced
3 eggs and 4 egg whites, well mixed
⅓ cup oil (grapeseed, safflower, or olive)

Combine all ingredients well. Lightly oil two 8"×10½" aluminum pans. Pour mixture into prepared pans and cover with foil. Place pans on cookie sheet. Bake covered for 1½ hours. Uncover the last 15 minutes of baking.

PASSOVER SOUR LEMON CAKE (PAREVE)

Preheat oven for 325°F.

1 cup cake meal
¼ cup potato starch
1⅓ cup sugar (save ¼ cup for egg whites)
½ teaspoon salt
4 egg yolks
8 egg whites
1 tablespoon lemon rind
⅓ cup lemon juice—add water to make ¾ cup liquid
1 teaspoon Passover baking powder
½ cup Passover grapeseed oil

Beat the 8 egg whites in the large mixing bowl until soft peaks are formed. Gradually add ¼ cup sugar, beating until stiff but not dry. Set aside. Combine dry ingredients (including remaining sugar) in large mixing bowl. Make a depression in the center of the dry ingredients. Add egg yolks, lemon juice water, lemon rind, and oil. Beat thoroughly in mixer (using unwashed beaters from egg whites) for 5 minutes. Fold one-third of beaten egg whites into yolk batter. Fold batter into remaining egg white mix. Splash warm water into ungreased bundt pan; shake out excess water. Put batter into wet pan; smooth top. Bake for 50–55 minutes until cake tester in center comes out clean, top is golden brown, and top of cake is springy to touch. Immediately invert pan upside down until cool. Go around outside and inside edges with knife. Invert onto a plate and glaze.

Glaze

3 tablespoons lemon juice
1 teaspoon lemon rind
1 tablespoon water

1 cup Passover confectioners sugar (If you can't find, put 1 cup less 1½ teapoons granulated sugar in food processor and process until very fine. Sift together with 1½ teaspoons potato starch.)

When cake is cool, poke holes in cake with toothpick so glaze can be absorbed. Spoon glaze over cake. Cake can be frozen or covered and stored in a cool place.

Passover Chocolate Nut Torte (Pareve)

Preheat oven to 350°F.

8 egg whites and 1 egg yolk
1 cup finely chopped walnuts
2 Red Delicious apples, peeled and finely chopped
1¼ cup sugar (reserve ¼ cup for egg whites)

2½ tablespoon grapeseed oil
6–8 tablespoons cocoa
1 teaspoon vanilla
½ teaspoon Passover baking powder, optional
½ cup matzah cake flour

Lightly oil a 9-inch round 3-inch deep springform pan. Trace around pan on wax paper with a pencil and cut out; line pan with wax paper. Beat 5 egg whites until stiff but not dry. Add ¼ cup sugar to egg whites a little at a time. Put beaten egg whites aside. In a clean bowl, beat egg yolk and 3 egg whites with 1 cup of sugar and oil until thick. Gently stir in nuts, cocoa, apple, and cake meal. Fold beaten egg whites into yolk mixture. Turn into springform pan. Bake 45 minutes or until cake springs back when touched. Cool in pan on wire rack. Run knife around torte and remove sides. Turn torte upside down onto plate; remove bottom. Cake will sink as it cools. It can be frozen now or glazed. Cake's texture is enhanced by freezing.

Glaze

3 oz. Kosher for Passover chocolate
3 tablespoons water
3 tablespoons sugar

2 tablespoons Kosher for Passover unsalted margarine

Combine all ingredients in a small pan. Heat over low heat, stirring until smooth and chocolate is melted. Slowly spoon over torte allowing glaze to drip down the sides.

Almond Clusters (Pareve)

Preheat oven to 350°F.

¾ pound (12 oz.) sliced almonds ⅔ cup sugar
2 egg whites

Line baking sheets with parchment paper. With large spoon, combine the egg whites and sugar without beating the egg whites. Add the almond slices and mix well. Drop by heaping teaspoonfuls onto parchment-lined baking pans. Bake 5 to 6 minutes; turn off oven; do not open oven door. Leave cookies in oven until oven cools. Peel clusters off paper and put in freezer bag. May be served right out of freezer. These are a Passover favorite.

Variations: (1) Add ⅔ cup finely chopped assorted candied fruit. (2) Melt 1 cup chopped chocolate or chocolate chips, and spread on bottom of cookies.

You can do this for either the fruit or nonfruit kind, but when you combine the variations, you get a mock florentine cookie. The better the chocolate you use, the better the cookie.

Passover Mandelbread (Pareve)

Preheat oven to 350°F.

¼ cup kosher for Passover grapeseed or safflower oil
¼ cup kosher for Passover margarine
1 egg and 3 egg whites
1¼ cup sugar
1 tablespoon kosher for Passover vanilla
1¾ cup matzah cake flour
¼ cup potato starch
½ teaspoon baking soda
½ teaspoon cream of tartar
Pinch of salt
⅓–½ cup kosher for Passover chocolate chips
Cinnamon and sugar

Lightly oil an 11½"×16½" cookie sheet. Place oil, margarine, egg and whites, sugar, and vanilla in food processor. Process until well mixed, about 25 seconds. Add rest of ingredients except chocolate chips to food processor and process with several on/off turns, just until flour is blended into dough. Add chocolate chips and process just until mixed with on/off turns. Spoon out mixture onto cookie sheet into two long rolls, shaping with a spatula. Bake on upper rack of oven for 25 minutes. Remove from oven, cut into slices, turn each slice on its side, and sprinkle each slice with a mixture of cinnamon and sugar. Return to oven and bake 10–12 minutes. Repeat process on the other side. Turn off oven and leave in another 10 minutes. Remove from cookie sheet and cool on wire rack. Store in air-tight plastic ziplock bag with all air removed. Mandelbread keeps at room temperature for a week. Can be frozen for later use.

Personal Reflections

Please use these empty pages to personalize **The New Traditonal Egalitarian Passover Haggadah** with reflections and inspirational passages of your own choosing.